D0669794

To Tim

★ FORTY ★

TONY VALENTE

Path to

Radiance

CONTENTS

CHAPTER 5
- FANTASIA -
005

CHAPTER 6
- JEAN PEDROVITCH OF NOCHE SALOMON GRISPÉPIN WONDERSMITH -
025

CHAPTER 7
- WELCOME TO RUMBLE TOWN -
045

CHAPTER 8
- NORTHERN SUBURB -
065

CHAPTER 9
- A THEATER PIECE -
085

CHAPTER 10
- DOMITOR -
105

CHAPTER 11
- TWO LOOGIES AND SOME PEE -
125

CHAPTER 12
- HERE COMES A NEW CHALLENGER! -
145

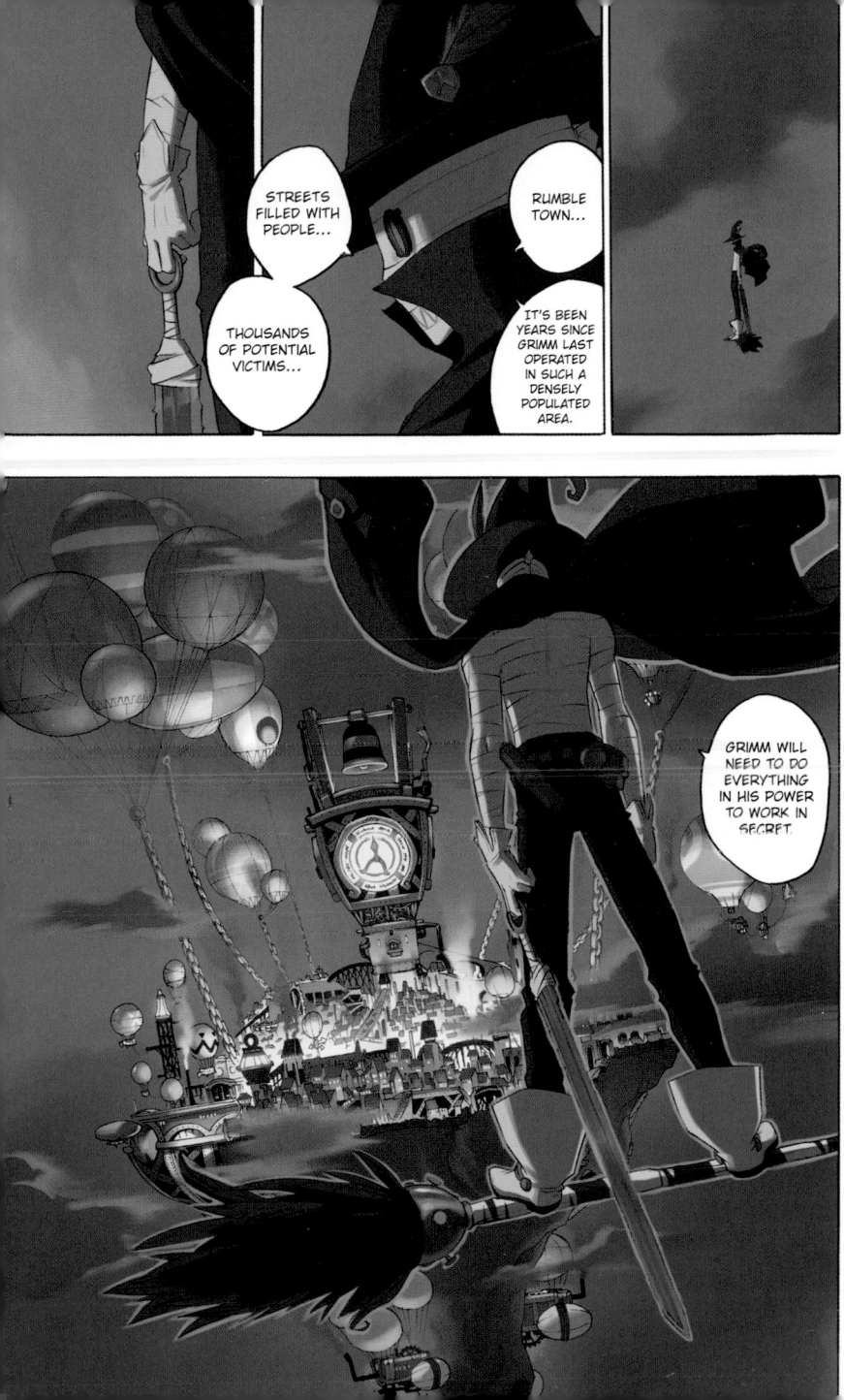
STREETS FILLED WITH PEOPLE...
RUMBLE TOWN...
THOUSANDS OF POTENTIAL VICTIMS...
IT'S BEEN YEARS SINCE GRIMM LAST OPERATED IN SUCH A DENSELY POPULATED AREA.
GRIMM WILL NEED TO DO EVERYTHING IN HIS POWER TO WORK IN SECRET.

Chapter 5
Fantasia

?
MR. SETH'S BELONGINGS?

FJHHHH
H H H
stage
B
Setting: Ruins
THE PROGRESS YOU'VE MADE IN THE LAST TWO WEEKS IS DAZZLING, MY BOY!
YA THINK SO?
HFF HFF
...A GOAT.
A GOAT?!
YEAH, AN OLD GOAT.
FEEBLE ...
...AND SHAKY.
BUT LOOK AT YOU NOW! YOU'D HAVE NO PROBLEM MEASURING UP AGAINST...
ABSOLUTELY! WHEN YOU FIRST ARRIVED HERE YOU WERE BARELY ABLE TO BLOW AWAY A SNAIL WITH A BLAST OF FANTASIA.

I'M SURE ALMA'S TOLD YOU THIS A THOUSAND TIMES ALREADY, BUT THE INQUISITION WILL PUT A GIANT TARGET ON YOUR BACK IF YOU'RE NOT CAREFUL ABOUT USING FANTASIA WITH YOUR BARE HANDS. YOU NEED TO LEARN TO CONFORM TO CONVENTIONAL PRACTICES IF YOU WANT TO AVOID ATTRACTING ATTENTION.
IF YOU WORK HARD, YOU SHOULD BE ABLE TO GO UP AGAINST A NEMESIS IN THE NEXT, SAY, YEAR OR TWO.
DON'T FORGET– I FIGURED OUT YOUR LITTLE TRICK RIGHT FROM THE START.
THAT MIGHT WORK WITH THE GULLIBLE BUMPKINS BACK IN POMPO HILLS, BUT YOU WON'T FOOL ANYONE WHO KNOWS WHAT TO LOOK FOR.
OH YEAH...
IT'S ALL BECAUSE OF THIS STUPID GLOVE–IT'S HOLDING ME BACK! IT SUCKS! I'M JUST GONNA GO BACK TO MY FLASK TRICK!
I'LL JUST PRETEND TO DRINK A MAGIC POTION, AND PROBLEM SOLVED!
COUNT YOURSELF LUCKY! THAT'S A REASONABLE TIME SPAN COMPARED TO OTHER WIZARD APPRENTICES!
I CAN'T WAIT *THAT* LONG TO GO LOOK FOR RADIANT!!
ONE OR TWO YEARS?!
I'VE ALREADY LOST ENOUGH TIME!
I DON'T CARE! THAT'S WAY TOO LONG!
WIIIIIIIIIZZ

HAA-AA!!
AND YOUR ATTACK LACKS FOCUS. YOU REALLY DIDN'T LISTEN TO A WORD I SAID, DID YOU?!
YOUR FANTASIA IS SPREAD TOO THIN.
BROOM BUMP !!
I'LL GIVE YOU THIS, BOY...
WHEN IT COMES TO TAKING A BEATING, YOU'RE A REAL HERO!
BUT HITTING ME IS A WHOLE DIFFERENT STORY.

LET'S TAKE IT FROM THE TOP THEN.
AND CONSIDERING EVERYTHING I ATE THIS MORNING, IT'LL BE MORE LOOK LIKE A TSUNAMI—
I DON'T WANNA HEAR THAT!
SECOND, YOU'RE MAKING ME DIZZY! I'M GOING TO PUKE!
STOP RUNNING ALL OVER THE PLACE!
FIRST OFF, YOU'LL JUST TIRE YOURSELF OUT—IT'S USELESS!

THAT ALL HAS TO DO WITH EXPERIENCE, MY BOY.
I'VE NEVER SEEN ALMA FLAIL AROUND LIKE THIS...

START WITH MAKING BIG MOVEMENTS TO GATHER AS MUCH FANTASIA AS POSSIBLE.

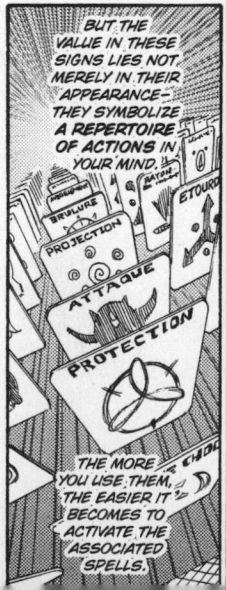
BUT THE VALUE IN THESE SIGNS LIES NOT MERELY IN THEIR APPEARANCE—THEY SYMBOLIZE A REPERTOIRE OF ACTIONS IN YOUR MIND.
BRULURE
PROJECTION
ATTAQUE
PROTECTION
THE MORE YOU USE THEM, THE EASIER IT BECOMES TO ACTIVATE THE ASSOCIATED SPELLS.

THAT CONCENTRATED FANTASIA WILL HELP CHANNEL YOUR WILL—YOUR INTENTION!
WIZARDS ASSOCIATE EACH OF THEIR INTENTIONS WITH A CERTAIN SIGN.
ANIMALS, EMBLEMS, OBJECTS, IDEOGRAMS, SYMBOLS...

NEXT, CONCENTRATE ALL THE ACCUMULATED ENERGY INTO A SINGLE POINT. THAT'S THE PART YOU KEEP OVERLOOKING, YET IT'S THE MOST CRUCIAL!!
GAH... I CAN'T...

YOU WILL HAVE TO CREATE YOUR OWN SIGN REPERTOIRE!
A SPIRAL SOMETHING. A WILD ANIMAL TO ATTACK. PERHAPS A SHIELD WHEN YOU WANT TO PROTECT YOURSELF? ASSOCIATE IMAGES THAT RESONATE WITH YOU TO YOUR WILL!
WHAT'S WITH THAT AWFUL-LOOKING SQUIGGLE?!
IS THAT REALLY EVERYTHING YOU'VE GOT?!
METEOR DROPS !!
BLOP
BLOP
BLOP
EASIER SAID THAN DONE!
COUNTER?
I'VE GOT NOTHING HERE!
COUNTER ALREADY!! YOU WON'T BE ABLE TO DODGE FOREVER!!
VROOOO

FINALLY, SOMETHING WE CAN WORK WITH!
NOW! PLAYTIME'S OVER! STAY LIKE THAT AND TRY COUNTERING THIS!
THIS FEELING!
IT'S JUST LIKE WHEN I'M NOT WEARING MY GLOVES!
THERE!
CAULDRON ...
I GATHER FANTASIA...
WUUUSHHHHHHH
... CRUSH !!!
...CONCENTRATE IT, AND...

...
FIW
?!!
Wush

?

Stage
B
Setting: Ruins
ALL RIGHT, BREAK TIME!
COME SEE ME AGAIN IN A FEW HOURS!

YOU DON'T GET IT... MY GLOVE EXPLODED! IT WAS THE ONLY ONE I HAD!
THAT'S NOTHING TO *WHINE* ABOUT! JUST GET YOURSELF A NEW ONE.
...I BARELY HAVE ENOUGH TO COVER ONE FINGER!
WITH THE LITTLE MONEY ALMA GAVE ME...

BWIT
BWIT
AAAAAAAH...
SURE, GO AHEAD AND CRY, MY BOY.
COLLECTING ALL THAT FANTASIA YET BEING UNABLE TO DO ANYTHING WITH IT... I'D DEFINITELY BE KICKING MYSELF OVER SOMETHING LIKE THAT IF I WERE YOU!

HA HA HA...! AAAH... I'M SO HAPPY TO SEE YOU AGAIN!
I DON'T GET A LOT OF VISITORS, YOU SEE. MY FITS MAKE ME... WELL, YOU KNOW. ENOUGH TALKING ABOUT ME! HOW WAS YOUR HOLIDAY IN VALLADINE–

...
SEEEETH... HA! HA!

HURRY !!
WAIT, SETH?!

MÉLIE? YOU THERE?
YES! I MEAN... NO! I MEAN, ONE MINUTE PLEASE!

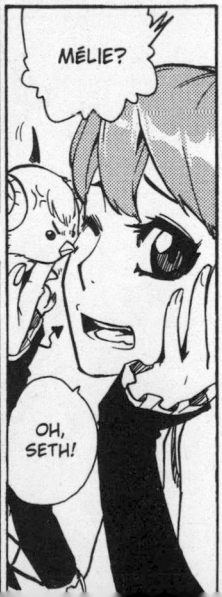
MÉLIE?
OH, SETH!

THAT GUY'S COMPLETELY FLAT!!

N-NO, NO! I'M FREE NOW! I-IT'S FINE!
HA HA...

UMM...
SHOULD I COME BACK TOMORROW WHEN YOU'RE LESS BUSY?

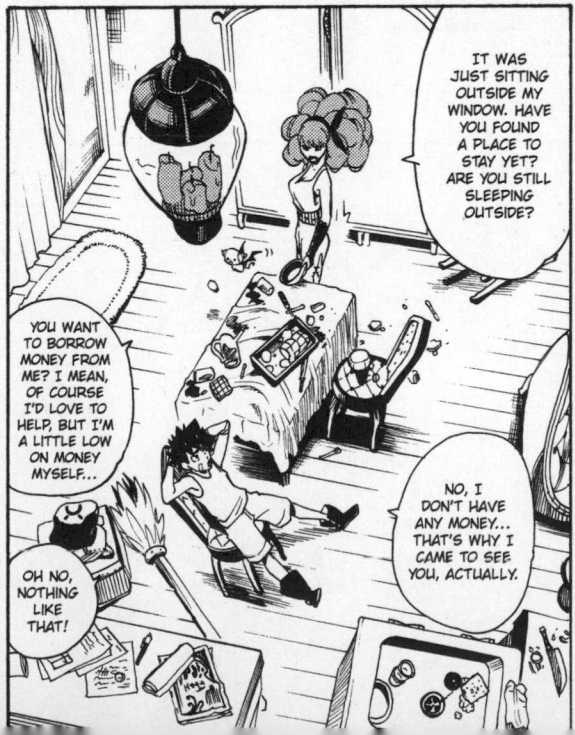
IT WAS JUST SITTING OUTSIDE MY WINDOW. HAVE YOU FOUND A PLACE TO STAY YET? ARE YOU STILL SLEEPING OUTSIDE?
YOU WANT TO BORROW MONEY FROM ME? I MEAN, OF COURSE I'D LOVE TO HELP, BUT I'M A LITTLE LOW ON MONEY MYSELF...
OH NO, NOTHING LIKE THAT!
NO, I DON'T HAVE ANY MONEY... THAT'S WHY I CAME TO SEE YOU, ACTUALLY.

OH, YOU HAVE MY STUFF? GREAT!
I LEFT EARLY THIS MORNING AND FORGOT TO TAKE IT WITH ME...

I'M IN A REALLY TIGHT SPOT RIGHT NOW!
WAIT, NO, YOU DON'T GET IT! I NEED TO FIND WORK!
NO GLOVE, NO PLACE TO STAY, NO FOOD...
I HAVE NO FRIENDS...
WE COULD EVEN HAVE LONG FRIENDLY LAUGHS LIKE, "HA HA HA!" OR, "HO HO HO!" WHICHEVER YOU PREFER!!
HERE, LET'S SETTLE ON A DATE, AND JOT IT DOWN IN YOUR PLANNER NOW!
OH, YOU'D LIKE TO USE MY SPARE BEDROOM?! LET ME THINK ABOUT IT–OKAY, DONE!
NOW WE'LL BE ABLE TO HAVE LONG TALKS WITH EACH OTHER AND EAT LONG LUNCHES AND GO ON LONG WALKS!!
...OR PARTNER UP WITH A WIZARD WHO COLLECTS INFORMATION AND CLUES THAT LEAD YOU TO A NEMESIS–AN INFORMANT.
TRAVEL THE WORLD AND LOOK FOR THEM ON YOUR OWN...
YOU SEE, THERE'S TWO WAYS TO HUNT NEMESES.
NEMESIS NEARBY.
ON OUR WAY!
WHERE IS IT?
THEY TRAVEL WITH TRACKERS AND RELAY MISSIONS AS THEY FIND CLUES.
AN INN FOR MEN? YOU MEAN I CAN'T STAY HERE?
HAVE YOU FOUND AN INFORMANT YET?
NO, NOT THAT!
I'M ACTUALLY HIS ONLY CLIENT.
DOC WORKS A COUPLE OF JOBS TO SUPPORT HIMSELF. HE'S NOT REALLY A GOOD INFORMANT SO HE DOESN'T MAKE A LOT OF MONEY FROM THAT.
IF HE'S THAT BAD AT HIS JOB, THEN WHY DON'T YOU GET SOMEONE ELSE?
ISN'T HE A CLEANING WIZARD?
WELL, YEAH! IT'S DOC.
SO YOU GOT ONE TOO?
HE'S A RESEARCH WIZARD...
A RESEARCH CLEANING WIZARD!

NO WAY! I'M NOT A FREELOADER!
ARE YOU HUNGRY? HERE, I'M FULL!
RMBLLL...
NO REALLY!
I'M GOOD!
GRMBLL...
GRWLLL...
JUST A LITTLE!
GRMBLLLL...
NO KIDDING...
NOBODY WANTS TO WORK WITH ME ANYMORE!
YOU'RE GOING TO JOIN THE OTHERS!
H-HELP ME!

I'LL PAY YOU BACK!
ALL RIGHT, IF YOU INSIST! JUST THIS ONCE!
YOU SAY THAT EVERY DAY!
UH-HUH...

SHHHH...

stage
B
Setting: Ruins
HERE! JUST TRY NOT TO TURN THEM INTO CONFETTI THIS TIME!
GYMNASIUM
CAULDRON ...
I GIVE UP, I GIVE UP!!
YOU REALLY SUCK!
OH, TRUST ME! I KNOW THAT THE GLOVES WON'T HELP YOU AT ALL!
WHAT!? YOU SUCK, OLD MAN! MAYBE THE REASON I CAN'T MAKE IT WORK IS BECAUSE YOU'RE A BAD TEACHER!
I DON'T THINK LESS CLOTH WILL CHANGE ANYTHING...
FINGERLESS GLOVES?

WHEN YOU WERE ROTATING YOUR HANDS, AIR POOLED INSIDE YOUR GLOVE AND FANTASIA MANAGED TO REACH YOUR BARE HAND.
WHEN YOU WERE DODGING MY METEOR DROPS, SOMETHING CHANGED.

YOU FINALLY READY TO LISTEN?
"OLD MAN"...? I'LL HAVE YOU KNOW I'M BARELY 126 YEARS OLD, MEATHEAD!
YES, SIR!
ANY-WAY!

...MADE YOUR GLOVE EXPLODE!
YOU GATHERED A LARGE AMOUNT OF IT WHICH, ONCE CONCENTRATED ...

THAT'S BECAUSE YOU DIDN'T GATHER ANY FANTASIA WITH YOUR GLOVE, BOY.
AND WHEN YOU TRANSFERED IT TO YOUR GLOVE, ALMOST ALL OF IT DISAPPEARED.
IT WAS ALL GATHERING AROUND YOUR ARM.

I THINK YOU'RE RIGHT...
IT DID FEEL THE SAME AS NOT WEARING THEM.

YOU SHOULD BE ABLE TO FEEL THE FANTASIA ON THE TIPS OF YOUR FINGERS AT ALL TIMES, AND USE THAT NATURAL TALENT OF YOURS.
THOSE FINGERLESS GLOVES SHOULD HELP YOU BYPASS THAT PROBLEM.

EVERYONE KNOWS ABOUT THEM, SO YOU'LL FIT RIGHT IN! SOME PEOPLE WILL EVEN MISTAKE YOU FOR BEING A MUCH MORE EXPERIENCED WIZARD THAN YOU ACTUALLY ARE.
QUITE A NUMBER OF EXPERIENCED WIZARDS USE FINGERLESS GLOVES WITHOUT BURNING THEMSELVES.
LET'S GO, BOY!
AND THIS TIME, TRY AND SPEW SOMETHING OTHER THAN HOT AIR, WILL YOU?!

OH, GOOD HEAVENS! WHAT HAPPENED TO YOU, GUDULE?!

CHAPTER 6

JEAN PEDROVITCH OF NOCHE
SALOMON GRISPÉPIN WONDERSMITH

PLEASE
TAKE A TICKET
-1D-
MASTER LORD MAJESTY
NOW ACCEPTING ALL
YOUR COMPLAINTS
MONDAY: 10:32 AM - 11:04 AM
TUESDAY: 11:08 AM - 12:16 PM
WEDNESDAY: --------
THURSDAY: 9:63 AM - 10:05 AM
FRIDAY: 8:20 PM - 9:21 PM
SATURDAY: DREAM ON
SUNDAY: DITTO

I'M
74!
NUMBER
74!
CLING
ZZZZ

DUN
386
Waiting Time Is Estimated to be 18799546

NUMBER 74! WHERE ARE YOUR MANNERS??
I'M NUMBER 386!! I'M NOT GOING TO SPEND ETERNITY IN A WAITING ROOM!
IF THE OTHERS AREN'T HAPPY WITH THAT, I'LL JUST RIP UP THEIR TICKETS!
KBAM
M-L-M
WHAT DID YOU SAY YOUR NAME WAS?
YOU ARE COMPLETELY IN THE RIGHT FOR PASSING IN FRONT OF THE OTHERS. IT'S WRITTEN IN YOUR CONTRACT, AFTER ALL.
OH?
YOU WILL, OF COURSE, BE CHARGED A SLIGHT FEE FOR IT, BUT LET'S GET ON TO BRASS TACKS...
SETH!
I'LL JUST CALL YOU JEAN-PEDROVITCH.
ESSYTEA H. SEV?
THAT'S QUITE THE MOUTHFUL!
WAIT... SEV?
NO, SETH! S-E-T-H, SETH!

SO, JEAN-PEDROVITCH OF NOCHE, WHAT BRINGS YOU HERE?
I'M LOOKING FOR AN INFORMANT TO HELP ME LOOK FOR RADIAN-
THERE'S AN INFORMANT REGISTER.
YOU CAN FIND IT AT THE LIBRARY. IT'S THE BIGGEST ONE OUT THERE, YOU KNOW. AFTER PAPO LIORI'S. AND ENTRANCE IS ENTIRELY FREE!

LOOK, MY LITTLE BIRD, I'D LOVE TO BE ABLE TO HELP EVERY SINGLE MEMBER OF THE ARTEMIS! TRULY, I WOULD!
BUT DADDY CAN'T JUST IDLY SHIRK HIS DUTY!
I AM LIKE A FATHER OF A FAMILY, AND YOU ALL, MY YOUNG.
MY WORK SCHEDULE IS JUST TOO-

THE ENTRANCE YEAH! BUT YOU NEED TO PAY TO LEAVE!!
DETAILS, DETAILS...
AND FOR TOUCHING A BOOK! AND WHAT ABOUT THE RENT FOR THE CHAIRS TO SIT ON?!

I FOUND A BUNCH OF THEM!
BUT NONE OF THEM WANT ANYTHING TO DO WITH RADIANT!

CHEESE-PATTERNED BRIEFS, PERFECT FOR GETTING BACK RUBS!
SNAP
GOOD LUCK WITH YOUR INFORMANT, MY LITTLE BIRD!
I'M OUTTA HERE!

PERFECT TIMING! I JUST FINISHED UP HERE WITH JEAN-PEDROVITCH OF NOCHE SALOMON!
YOUR MASSEUSES ARE HERE, MASTER LORD MAJESTY!
HEY
HOLD ON!!

ZO...
OM

GET OFF!
HM, THESE HORNS ARE USEFUL!
GET OFF ME RIGHT NOW OR I'LL KICK YOUR BUTT, KITTY!
YOU'RE LOOKING FOR RADIANT?
WHAT THE HECK'RE YOU DOING IN BRIEFS ON MY HEAD?!
THW
AK
I TOLD YOU TO GET OFF-
YOU'RE REALLY NOT JOKING, ARE YOU?
...YOU ARE GOING TO HAVE A LOT OF DIFFICULTY FINDING SOMEONE TO HELP YOU.
...AND THOSE WHO'D RATHER NOT SPEND THEIR ENTIRE LIVES CHASING AFTER RAINBOWS...
BETWEEN THOSE WHO ONLY KIND OF BELIEVE IN IT...
THAT HURT...
I JUST KICKED MYSELF IN THE FACE.
LOOK, JEAN-PEDROVITCH OF NOCHE SALOMON GRISPÈPIN.
I DIDN'T ASK FOR YOUR SUPPORT, SO I DON'T CARE IF YOU DON'T BELIEVE ME OR AREN'T INTERESTED!
THE JOB IS ENORMOUS, AND THE GOAL IS TOO VAGUE...
AND FOR ALL YOU KNOW THERE'S MORE THAN ONE RADIANT OUT THERE!

COME BACK HERE WHEN YOU'VE MADE SOME PROGRESS. I MIGHT SHOW YOU MY GRATITUDE DEPENDING ON HOW USEFUL YOUR INFORMATION TURNS OUT TO BE.
OUR GOAL HERE AT THE ARTEMIS INSTITUTE IS TO FIND A CURE FOR THE INFECTIONS CAUSED BY NEMESES.
FINDING THE NEMESES' NEST, RADIANT, COULD LEAD US TO VERY INTERESTING LEADS IN THAT ENDEAVOR.
OH, BUT I AM INTERESTED!
FWOOP
TAC
REALLY ?
BY CUTTING IN FRONT OF 312 OF YOUR COMRADES, YOU ACCUMULATED ALL OF THEIR INDIVIDUAL DEBTS!
CF. ART. 422, PARAGRAPH B, SECTION 2...
JEAN-PEDROVITCH OF NOCHE SALOMON GRISPÉPIN WONDERSMITH
YOU'RE AHEAD OF everyone ON THE ARTEMIS HISTORICAL DEBT RANKING.
THAT'S WHY THEY WERE ALL LAUGHING LIKE THAT?!!
CONGRATULATIONS!!!
YAY
IDALGO SAINT-ANDRÉ
CHUCKBORIS ARMAGEDDON LUFTANSIO NORBERT
PÉLAGIE URSULINE ABÉMA
MR. HENRI KINGSLEY SIGASFRIN
ELFIE JOHN DUPONT MANCHADORE
BERNADOUILLE
MAILLE DINGDONG DONG
JINDRICHOVICE BIANCARÈLE FRIDA LALALA
WITH YOUR DEBT OF 39,373,256,211.93 DIMES, YOU'VE BROKEN THE PREVIOUS RECORD!
IN EXCHANGE FOR HAVING CUT IN FRONT OF EVERYONE ELSE WAITING–
OH, ONE LAST THING BEFORE YOU LEAVE.
A PIN?
I CHEAT AND I GET A PIN?!
SO I THOUGHT THIS TOKEN WOULD BE FITTING FOR YOUR ACTIONS TODAY.
YOU'RE WAY AHEAD OF EVERYONE ELSE NOW!
AHEAD OF WHAT, NOW?

DO YOU HAVE A BROTHER, SETH?
WHY?!
NAH!
AND ONE LAST THING!
WHAT ?!
A STATUE WILL BE PUT UP IN YOUR HONOR!
GLORY TO THE NEW CONQUEROR– THE VICTOR!
GLORY! GLORY!
YAY!
NO REASON. FORGET I ASKED.

Kettle Coffee
café cuit à la marmite
K.C.
Kettle Coffee
WELL HELLO, DOC!
IF ONLY SHE WASN'T ATTACHED TO HER FATHER, I WOULD'VE CONFESSED TO HER ALREADY!
WHAT A BEAUTY...
I'M TELLING YOU, THIS GUY IS DEFINITELY A LAZY OAF!
NOT LIKE HE'S GOT ANYTHING ELSE TO DO!!
YOU'RE HERE EARLY TODAY!
MISTER MELBA FATHER
IN AN ANONYMOUS LETTER...SENT FROM A FOREIGN COUNTRY...
FATHER! DON'T SAY THAT!
MISS MELBA
GREEN LIKE LETTUCE! BUT BABY LETTUCE...
BLAH BLAH BLAH...
CUTE BABY LETTUCE.
CULTIVATED IN PARADISE.
AAAH... SUCH A NICE COMPLEXION!
BLAH BLAH BLAH...
AND THOSE GREEN EYES. GREEN...

ALWAYS MAKING FUNNY JOKES!
HA HA HA! GOOD OL' DOC!
HA HA! YES, GOOD OL' ME! HA HA...
...
?
GULP!
I MEAN...
DOC?
WHAT CAN I GET YOU TO DRINK?
WHAT? UM... OH!
OH YES, YOU!
WOULD YOU LIKE ANYTHING ?
I WAS JUST THINKING OUT LOUD!!
YOU ASKED ME TO!
WHY'D YOU PINCH ME?!
I'M SO SORRY! I DIDN'T KNOW!! PLEASE FORGIVE ME!
FUU FUU!
I'M DONE!
NEVER!
FINISHED!
WHY DID I SAY THAT?!
I MUST BE DREAMING... YES, THAT'S IT! THIS IS A NIGHTMARE! I NEED TO WAKE UP! SOMEONE PINCH ME!
NOW SHE'LL NEVER TAKE ME SERIOUSLY!
AAAAAH!!!
UWAAAAAHH !!!

WHAT ABOUT THE MISSION YOU CONTACTED ME ABOUT?
I SENT YOU A RESPONSE A WEEK AGO, BUT I HAVEN'T HEARD ANY NEWS SINCE...
OFF YOU GO! SCRAM BEFORE ANOTHER ONE OF YOUR FITS GETS US BOTH KILLED!
WE ONLY COMMUNICATE VIA LETTERS!! SO DON'T GET COME ME!
WHAT ARE YOU DOING HERE ANYWAY?! WE HAD AN AGREEMENT, RIGHT?

I HAVEN'T BEEN ABLE TO GO BACK HOME BECAUSE OF HIM! I'M SURE HE WON'T BE ABLE TO FIND ME–
HE WON'T STOP TALKING ABOUT NEMESES AND RADIANT!
OH, RIGHT! THAT'S BECAUSE OF SETH... HE WON'T LEAVE ME ALONE!

DOC !!

DOC!
HFF
HFF
I WANT TO TEAM UP WITH YOU!
PLEASE LEAVE A MESSAGE.
DOC ISN'T AVAILABLE RIGHT NOW.
?
HFF

BRINGING BACK NEMESES IN BITS AND PIECES IS POINTLESS! I CAN'T GET ANYTHING OUT OF THOSE! HOW AM I SUPPOSED TO LIVE WITH THAT!?
I REFUSE TO EAT GRASS FOREVER!
I'M NOT BAD AT MY JOB! IT'S JUST THAT I TAKE TIME TO DO IT PROPERLY!
NEVER MIND THAT! I'M NOT WORKING WITH YOU!
BUT NOT YOU! HUFF... I'M LUCKY YOU'RE SO BAD AT YOUR JOB!
...AND THEY SAID THEY ALREADY HAVE TOO MANY WIZARDS TO MANAGE!
I CHECKED WITH THE OTHER INFORMANTS ...
WHY AM I THE ONLY ONE ATTRACTING THESE WEIRDOS?!
WEIRDOS...?

HOW ABOUT A TRIAL RUN THEN?!
IF I CAN GET YOU A LIVING NEMESIS, WILL YOU HELP ME?

PLEASE! YOU'RE THE ONLY ONE WHO'LL ANSWER MY QUESTIONS ABOUT RADIANT! EVEN IF YOU'RE BAD AT YOUR JOB, I STILL WANT YOU!
I AM NOT BAD AT MY JOB!!

YOU CAN'T JUST REFUSE LIKE THAT! I GAVE YOU MY TRADEMARK SERIOUS LOOK!
NEVER!
BUT...
AT LEAST THINK ABOUT IT!
NOPE!!
ALL RIGHT, HMM...
THIS! THE DETERMINED HERO LOOK!!
I SAID NO!!
...
NO.
PLUS...
HMM?
HE'S GOT SOME GOOD TRICKS UP HIS SLEEVE.
I SAW SETH AT WORK WITH MASTER YAGA...
A LIVING NEMESIS... THAT WOULD BE WORTH A LOT OF MONEY!
I HAVE TO SAY THAT I WOULDN'T BE AGAINST THE IDEA OF REFILLING OUR WALLETS A LITTLE BIT. YOU KNOW, WITH ALL THE BILLS TO PAY, MATERIALS TO BUY...
FRIENDS TO REPAIR...

MÉLIE, I'LL PAY YOU BACK FOR ALL THOSE MEALS!
THANKS!
ALL RIGHT, JUST THIS ONCE.
IF ONLY HE KNEW THAT BRINGING BACK A LIVING NEMESIS IS PRACTICALLY IMPOSSIBLE...
OH, NO NEED FOR THAT. I OWE YOU THAT MUCH FOR SAVING ME AFTER I GOT CAUGHT BY THE INQUISITION.
OH COME ON! JUST ONE TRY!
COULDN'T CARE LESS. THE KID'S GOT NOTHING BUT TROUBLE WRITTEN ALL OVER HIM.
I'LL EVEN GIVE YOU MY PIN!
AND IF IT DOESN'T WORK OUT, I SWEAR YOU'LL NEVER SEE ME AGAIN!
AND I'M A GREAT SENSOR! I'VE GOT A KNACK AT SENSING TROUBLE.
HMM?
CROSS MY HEART!
NEVER EVER?
"SHORT RECKONINGS MAKE LONG FRIENDS."
"LONG FRIENDS."
ALMA ALWAYS TOLD ME, "SHORT RECKONINGS MAKE LONG FRIENDS!"
I INSIST! I WOULDN'T HAVE HAD ANYTHING TO EAT IF IT WEREN'T FOR YOU!
NO REALLY, IT'S...

POT
?!
YES MA'AM!!
ALL RIGHT! THEN PAY ME BACK QUICKLY!
AH, FALSE ALARM–IT WASN'T ONE OF HER FITS.
!!
I DIDN'T MEAN TO DISRESPECT YOUR FRIENDS...
I AM SO SORRY, DOC!
OH, DON'T WORRY. THEY'RE NOT MY FRIENDS.
THEN WHAT'S A GIRL WITH A BOUNCY BUTT LIKE THAT DOING WITH A WARTHOG LIKE YOU?
PLEASE EXCUSE MY FATHER, HE BECOMES UNCONTROLLABLE WHEN HE'S IN HIS MOODS...
OH MY, FATHER! I DIDN'T KNOW YOU TO BE SO INDECENT!
BUT SHE'S THE HUSSY WHO'S BENT OVER THE TABLE!
I'M SO HUMILIATED... HELP ME...
THEY EVEN ZOOMED IN ON MY BUTT... I FEEL SO DIRTY...
FATHER, ENOUGH!
AAH... SHE'S SO CUTE WITH THAT INNOCENT LOOK AND THOSE PINK CHEEKS. PINK LIKE A NICE HAM, BUT HAM MADE FROM THE CUTEST BABY PIGS...
WAAAH!

IS THAT TRUE? YOU'RE GOING TO HUNT A NEMESIS, DOC?
YOU'RE SO BRAVE!
I DIDN'T KNOW YOU TO BE SO ADVENTUR-OUS!
WHOA, THERE! WHO SAID THAT? I ONLY LOOK FOR INFORMATION, AND IT'S YOU WHO HUNT–
WE WORK TOGETHER! ALL THREE OF US ARE GOING TO HUNT A NEMESIS!
BUT AREN'T YOU AFRAID OF THE NEMESES? I WOULD BE ABSOLUTELY TERRIFIED!
N-NO! I'M USED TO IT.
WE'RE ACTUALLY GOING TO CAPTURE ONE ALIVE.
Y-YOU THINK SO?
I MEAN, OF COURSE I'M BRAVE... IT'S THE ADVENTURER IN ME!
GULP!
...

SO WHERE ARE WE GOING TO FIND OURSELVES THIS NEMESIS??
WHAT DID I GET MYSELF INTO THIS TIME?!
IT'S NOT UGLY! IT'S CAMOUFLAGED SO WE DON'T ATTRACT ANY ATTENTION.
HEY, DOC! WHAT'S UP WITH THIS UGLY AIRSHIP BY THE WAY?
IT'S UGLY CAMOUFLAGE!
AND I HAVE YOU TO THANK FOR THE INQUISITION NOT FORGETTING ABOUT MY AIRSHIP ANYTIME SOON!
THEN OFF TO BUBBLE DOWN!
RUMBLE TOWN.
IT'S RUMBLE TOWN!
JUNGLE CLOWN.
...
I'VE ONLY BEEN THERE ONCE, BUT IT WAS FOR LONG ENOUGH TO KNOW THAT THE TOWNSPEOPLE THERE REALLY ARE NOT FOND OF WIZARDS.
HAIR-DRESSERS! THAT'S TOTALLY PLAUSIBLE WITH MÉLIE'S WILD RED HAIR!
I DON'T KNOW! HOW ABOUT...
THEN WHAT ARE WE?
AND HIDE YOUR HORNS!
FROM NOW ON, IF ANYONE ASKS—WE ARE NOT WIZARDS.
NOW GET IN HERE AND HIDE YOUR BROOM.

CAPTAIN! THAT AIRSHIP IS BACK!
AND, IT'S GROWN OUT IT'S MUSTACHE!!
IT SEEMS TO BE HEADED DOWN THE NORTHERN CURRENT! TO THE NORTHWEST!
POF
MALLEUS MALEFICARUM
NORTH-NORTHWEST ...
IF THEY'RE HEADED THAT WAY WITH A SMALL SHIP, THEN THERE'S ONLY ONE PLACE THEY COULD POSSIBLY BE GOING.

RELAY THIS MESSAGE TO GENERAL TORQUE– "I AM HEADED TO RUMBLE TOWN FOLLWOING THE TRAIL OF THE HORNED WIZARD..."
"...I SHALL AWAIT YOUR ORDERS AT LIEUTENANT KONRAD OF MARBOURG'S STATION.
SIGNED, ...YOUR LOYAL CAPTAIN, DRAGUNOV."

BRMM
BRMM
BRMM
BRMM

WHAT WAS IT LIKE BACK THEN, DOC?
HOW THE HELL SHOULD I KNOW?! DO YOU REALLY THINK I'M LIKE 300 YEARS OLD OR SOMETHING?!
I DUNNO... HOW OLD ARE YOU?

SO, WHAT'S RUMBLE TOWN LIKE?
IT'S NOT UGLY, BUT IT'S VERY NOISY.
AND IT ALSO SHAKES A LOT.
IT SMELLS.
IT'S ONE OF THE LAST REMNANTS OF THE INDUSTRIAL ERA.
ZZZZZ

THE TOWN'S NAME USED TO BE "PROSPERITY," BUT THE VILLAGERS EVENTUALLY RENAMED IT AFTER THE CONSTANT NOISE.
IT'S THE FACTORIES. WE'RE GETTING CLOSE.
KLANG
KLANG
KLANG
KLANG
NOW'S NOT THE TIME FOR A HISTORY LESSON ANYWAY!
YEAH, WHAT'S THAT NOISE?
HEAR THAT?
KLANG
KLANG
KLANG
KLANG
KLANG
KLANG
THE TOWN THAT ALWAYS RUMBLES.
RUMBLE TOWN.

VEAL ROAST.
BLARG
PLEASE, TAKE THIS AS AN APOLOGY FOR MY FATHER'S BEHAVIOR.
IT'S A BLEND I MADE MYSELF.
OHH! DELICIOUS! EXQUISITE!
T-THIS IS UNEX-PECTED! WHAT IS IT?

Chapter 7
Welcome to Rumble Town

LET'S LAND HERE. NOBODY'S GOING TO COME BOTHER US.
THE PORT IS DE-SERTED!
DONG
DONG
KLANG
KLANG
DONG
KLANG
KRANK

DONG
WE WERE CONTACTED BY A FAMILY OF WORKISTS.
IT'S ERS.
THEY LIVE IN THE NORTHERN SUBURB.
WORKIS-TERS.

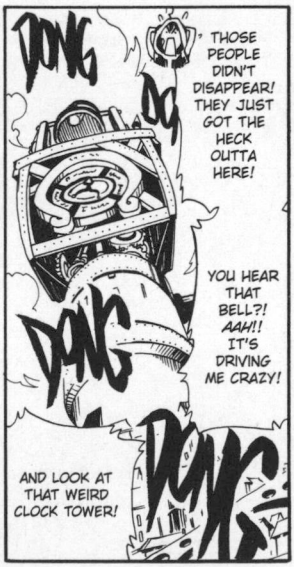
DONG
THOSE PEOPLE DIDN'T DISAPPEAR! THEY JUST GOT THE HECK OUTTA HERE!
YOU HEAR THAT BELL?! AAH!! IT'S DRIVING ME CRAZY!
DONG
AND LOOK AT THAT WEIRD CLOCK TOWER!
DONG

OVER THE LAST FEW WEEKS THERE'S BEEN A HANDFUL OF CASES OF PEOPLE MYSTERIOUSLY DISAPPEARING.
WHAT DOES THE NEMESIS LOOK LIKE?
NO INFOR-MATION ON THAT YET.
DONG
DONG
NO WITNESSES? EVEN IN SUCH A CROWDED TOWN?

THIS PLACE HAS EYES AND EARS EVERY-WHERE. RUMBLE TOWN IS THE MOST POPULATED ISLET IN THE ENTIRE REGION!
JUST A QUICK WORD OF ADVICE-DON'T DO ANYTHING EXTRAVA-GRAZY! ONE WRONG MOVE AND WE'LL HAVE THE INQUISITION AFTER US!

DONG
DONG
DONG
WOO
OSH

GRRRR!
THERE'S LITERALLY NOBODY HERE!
THAT'S REALLY DARK! WE'RE GONNA GET CURSED!
MAYBE THEY ALL DIED!
...
I GUESS EVERYONE'S OUT TO LUNCH?
THERE'S A CAT...
HEY KITTY!

HA! HA!
I'M SORRY, MR. CAT!
...
DON'T LEAVE ME HANGING, MAN...
HEY! YOU'RE STRONGER THAN I THOUGHT! HIGH FIVE!
OH! LOOK AT THAT MEAN CAT DEATH LOCK!
LET HIM GO!
TAP
TAP
MISTER BOOBRIE!!
MEE-OWW !!
!!
?
HMM...
WHAT'S WRONG, DOC?
I, UH...
I-I JUST SUDDENLY GOT THIS SPLITTING HEADACHE... IT'S AS IF...

LET'S FOLLOW IT AND SET A TRAP!
BAD! THAT'S BAD!
IT'S GONE... IT MUST NOT HAVE NOTICED US...
GOOD! THAT'S GOOD!
THE NEMESIS!
STEP
STEP
LET ME START WITH THIS TRASH BIN!
GO AHEAD, I'LL STAY AROUND HERE AND SEE IF I CAN FIND ANYONE...
WIZZ
FUHHH
BOM!!

WE'VE GOTTA HURRY OR WE'LL LOSE IT!
THEN I'LL JUST ATTACK IT MYSELF!
BUT IF WE GET TOO CLOSE, WE MIGHT LOSE THE ELEMENT OF SURPRISE!
IT'LL HAVE TO SLOW DOWN TO FIGHT ME!
IN THE MEANTIME, YOU JUST WAIT FOR THE RIGHT MOMENT TO–

KLUM
HOW'D HE DO THAT?!
IT WAS SUDDENLY WAY AHEAD OF US!
THAT'S NOT THE ONE WE WERE CHASING.
...THEN DOC'S DEFINITELY GOING TO WANT TO WORK WITH ME!
IF WE GET TWO LIVING ONES...
!!
LOOK, THE OTHER ONE'S BACK!
THERE'S TWO OF THEM?!
AND THEY LOOK IDENTICAL.

...
SETH?
IF WE CONTINUE MOVING DOWN HERE THIS FAST WE'LL JUST END UP FLYING STRAIGHT INTO A WALL. LET'S GET A LITTLE HIGHER UP AND FOLLOW THEM FROM ABOVE.
WHAT'S WRONG WITH THEM?!
IT LOOKS LIKE THEY'RE RESPONDING TO SOME KIND OF SIGNAL.
FUZZ

JUST HOW MANY OF THEM ARE THERE?!
RUN

WEIRD... EVEN FALLING ON THEM DOESN'T GET THEIR ATTENTION...
HEEEEEY !!!
WOOSHH
...
MAYBE THEY'VE BEEN HYPNO-TIZED?
LOOK HERE! I'M SPITTING ON YOU! PTOO!!
YOU DON'T CARE?!
GRAK! PTOO!
PTOOOO!!
...
WELL...
JUST SHOW ME WHERE YOU'RE HEADED THEN.

!!
VERON!
SOM!

PERFECT... NOBODYS HERE TO BOTHER US.
SHHHH ...
WHAT'S UP WITH THIS ISLET FROM HELL?!
ARE YOU FOR REAL?!
JUST LEAVE THE QUESTIONS TO GRIMM, LITTLE BOY.
ARE YOU NUTS? WHAT THE HECK DO YOU WANT? I'LL KICK YOUR BUTT!

GRIMM URGES YOU TO THINK REAL HARD...
...AND RECONSIDER ANSWERING HIM IN MORE DETAIL.
SOMEONE CALLED YOU, DIDN'T THEY?
SHUT UP!
WHAT ARE YOU AND YOUR LITTLE FRIENDS DOING SKULKING AROUND THIS PLACE?
I'M NOT GOING TO TELL YOU ANYTHING!
LOOKS LIKE YOU DIDN'T HEAR ME...
WHAT ARE YOU DOING IN RUMBLE TOWN?

TAKE OUT A CANNON FROM YOUR UNDER-WEAR FOR ALL I CARE...
HMM ...
ANOTHER UNCLEAR ANSWER...
...I HAVE NOTHING MORE TO TELL YOU, TOILET-PAPER FACE.
REPELL!!

METEOR DROPS!!
BLOP
BLOP
FSHH
FSHH
FSHHHH
THUNK
PROCELLA— THE STORM!
SWF

BROOM
HE'S FAST...
HE CHARGES UP HIS ATTACKS WAY TOO FAST, WITH THAT SWORD OF HIS TWIRLING ALL OVER THE PLACE.
AGH...
HE'S NOT GIVING ME THE TIME TO COLLECT ENOUGH FANTASIA.
THIS IS BAD!
"MY BOY! WHEN YOU WERE ROTATING YOUR HANDS..."
DOP
FSHIIII
"...A LARGE AMOUNT OF FANTASIA GATHERED UNDER YOUR GLOVES."
THAT'S IT...!

SKULL POKE!!
VENE CIUM REVELARE— MAGIC REVEAL!
KBR OM

FSHH+++
HEY!
YOUR LITTLE FRIENDS WILL CERTAINLY HAVE BEEN ALERTED BY ALL THE NOISE.
GRIMM IS A SHY MAN. HE MUST TAKE HIS LEAVE NOW.
DON'T JUST LEAVE!!
WHIZ
...AND TREAT THEM TO THE TIP OF HIS BLADE.
DON'T WORRY, GRIMM WILL MEET THEM SOON ENOUGH...
I'M NOT DONE WITH YOU!

GRRRR!

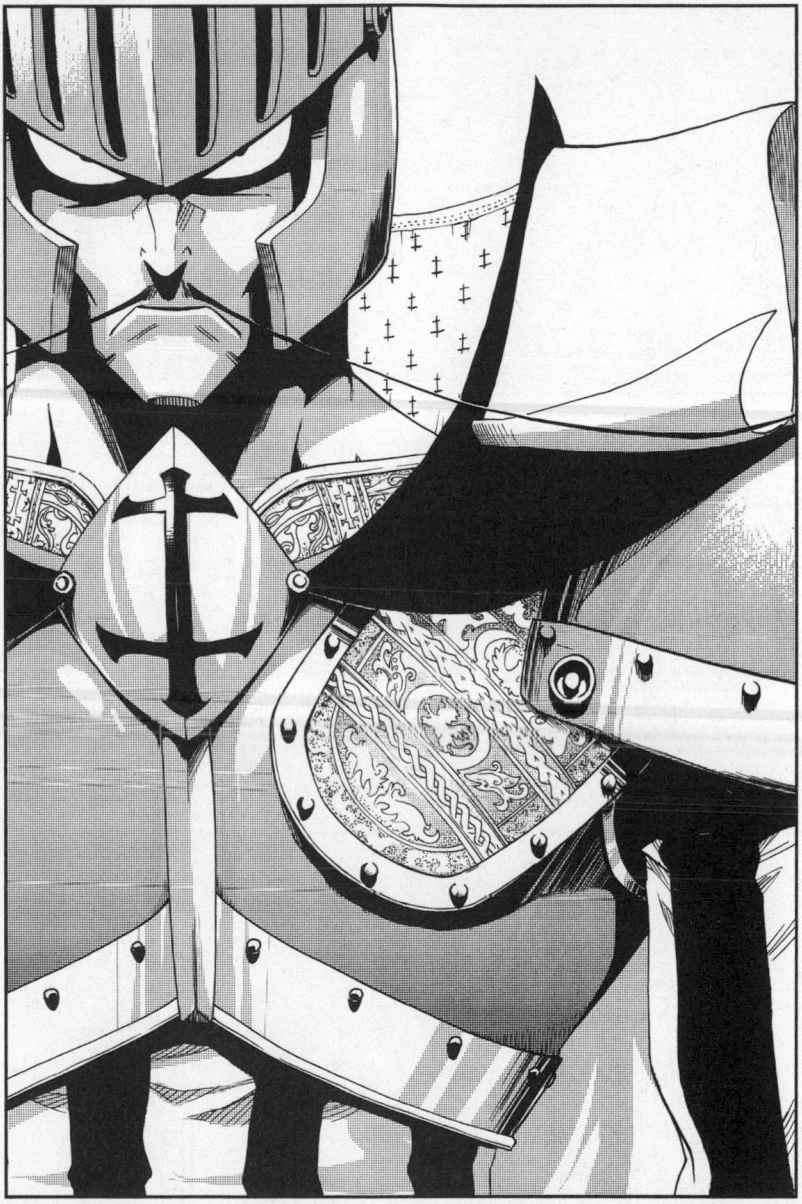

CHAPTER 8

NORTHERN SUBURB

SHF
WE CAN'T! THE STREETS ARE FILLED WITH PEOPLE EVER SINCE THE CLOCK STOPPED RINGING. EVERYONE WILL SEE US!!
I'LL EXPLAIN LATER! WE NEED TO FIND DOC, HE'S IN DANGER! GET YOUR BROOM, I LOST MINE!
WAS THAT EXPLOSION YOUR FAULT?
MÉLIE! YOU'RE STILL IN ONE PIECE!!
CRAP! START RUNNING!!

DOC?!
DOC!!

OH, DOC...
AT LEAST HE'S ALIVE.

YOU IDIOTS!
SAVE ME...
HEY, I THINK THIS 'ERE SQUASH JUST SAID SOME-THIN'...
AND THESE SAUSA-GES'RE MOVIN'!
OBVIOUSLY A LITTLE PIG GOT CAUGHT IN THE MESS!

DOC!!
HE WAS HERE! DOC!!
DOC!!

THAT BASICALLY DESCRIBES MOST OF THEM OUT THERE.
HM, SO JUST YOUR RUN-OF-THE-MILL WIZARD...
HE WAS WEARING A HAT AND A LONG COAT DANGLING FROM HIS SHOULDERS.
SO YOU'RE SAYING HE'S AFTER US? WHAT'D HE LOOK LIKE?
NO, NOT TWO.
T-TWO?!
GOOD ...
TA-DAAA!
NOPE!
OH! AND HE LOOKED LIKE A GIANT ROLL OF TOILET PAPER AND HAD A SWORD COMING OUT OF HIS HAND!
BUT THE TWO NEMESES ESCAPED.
I COUNTED AT LEAST FIFTEEN!
?!
THEY ROAM THE AREA IN SEARCH OF AN IDEAL SPOT FOR THE SOURCE NEMESIS TO CAUSE THE MOST DAMAGE.
NEMESES ARE KNOWN TO SOMETIMES FALL DOWN ACCOMPANIED BY WHAT WE CALL ECHO NEMESES.
SOURCE NEMESIS
ECHO NEMESES
THEY'RE SMALLER, LESS POWERFUL AND MORE DISCREET-BASICALLY THEY ACT AS SCOUTS.
THAT CONFIRMS MY SUSPICIONS. THOSE WERE ECHOES.
EGGOS?
FIFTEEN ...

AN INQUISITOR PATROL!
WHAT ARE THEY DOING HERE?
!!
H-HIDE!
HOW INTERESTING ...!
ALMA USED TO CALL THEM DROPPINGS.
OH, I KNOW THOSE!
!

SO MUCH SO THAT THEY'VE BECOME SUBSTITUTES FOR MILITIAS ON CERTAIN ISLETS.
EVER SINCE THE INQUISITION ORGANIZED ITSELF INTO AN ARMY, IT'S BECOME EXTREMELY INFLUENTABLE!
YOU MEAN FLUENTIAL?
WHATEVER, IT'S GOT A LOT OF INFLUENCE!

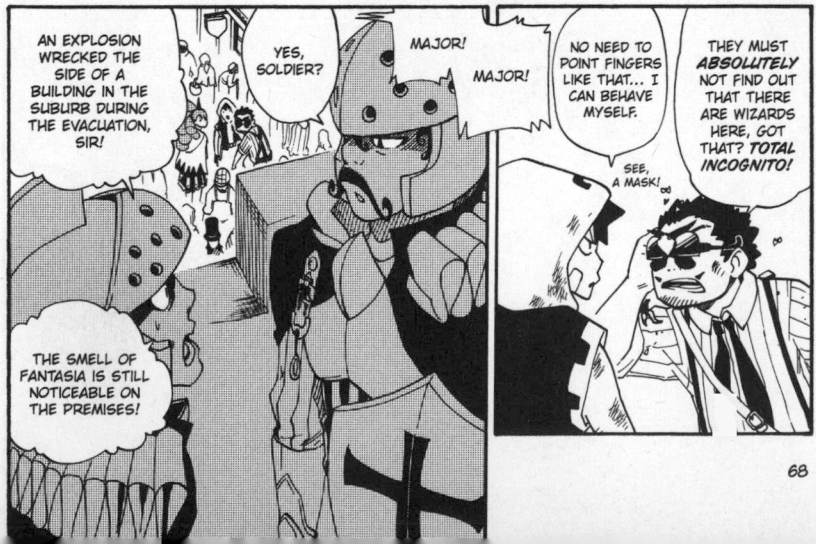
AN EXPLOSION WRECKED THE SIDE OF A BUILDING IN THE SUBURB DURING THE EVACUATION, SIR!
YES, SOLDIER?
MAJOR!
MAJOR!
THE SMELL OF FANTASIA IS STILL NOTICEABLE ON THE PREMISES!
NO NEED TO POINT FINGERS LIKE THAT... I CAN BEHAVE MYSELF.
SEE, A MASK!
THEY MUST ABSOLUTELY NOT FIND OUT THAT THERE ARE WIZARDS HERE, GOT THAT? TOTAL INCOGNITO!

-RUMBLE TOWN-
NORTHERN SUBURB

NOK NOK!!

BAM
PWI!
YES, HELLO?
SHE'S HAVING A FIT? NOW?!
PWII!
GET LOST, BOOBRIE!
A LITTLE PATIENT-ISM, MR. DESTROYER OF PROPERTY!
CAN THEY HURRY UP ALREADY?
I DIDN'T SAY THAT!

MISS ZEHD?
HMMM...
PWIIII...

OH, VISITORS I SEE, MISS ZEHD?
HELLO, MISS ZEHD!
HERE'S YOUR MAIL, MISS ZEHD.

AH...
NO, YOU MUST BE MISTAKEN.

THANK YOU.
BUT I HAVE TO ADMIT THAT WITH YOUR APPEARANCE AND THAT SMELL OF HIS...
KIDS, I DON'T WANT TO HEAR THOSE VULGARITIES FROM YOU!
GOAT-HORNED PUNKERS!
I'M SO SORRY, I THOUGHT YOU WERE...
BEGGARS?
DRUGGIES!
SMELLOBIS!
BUMS!
THE ZEHD FAMILY
LET ME FIRST THANK YOU ALL FOR RESPONDING TO OUR REQUEST.
WE REALLY DIDN'T KNOW WHO ELSE TO TURN TO.
WE'RE LUCKY YOUR ARMS ARE SO BIG! I WOULDN'T HAVE BEEN ABLE TO STOP HER ON MY OWN!
AND THE ONE ABOUT TO PUNCH MY KIDS?
OH, SORRY ABOUT THAT. HE'S A CLEANING WIZARD!
PWUH!
WHAT WAS THAT?!

OR SO HE PRETENDS! NO ONE ELSE WAS THERE TO SEE IT HAPPEN! AAAH! THAT BRAT.
MY APOLOGIES. A NEMESIS.
THEY'RE CALLED NEMESES!
ONE OF OUR SONS FELL VICTIM TO A MONSTER DURING AN EVACUATION AFTER WE LOST SIGHT OF HIM.

WE EVACUATE WHENEVER THE DRILLING RISKS CAUSING A CERTAIN AREA TO COLLAPSE.
IT'S BECAUSE THE ISLET'S UNSTABLE.

WE TRIED TO LOOK FOR IT IN THE SUBURBS, BUT YOU KNOW HOW OUR EVACUATIONS WORK?
THANKS, HONEY.
NOW, NOW, DEARY, CALM DOWN. HERE, HAVE SOME TEA.
ACTUALLY, WE DON'T. WHY DO YOU HAVE THESE EVACUATIONS?

THOSE BENT NEEDLES POINT TO THE AREAS THAT NEED TO EVACUATE WHILE THE STRAIGHT ONE POINTS TO THE PLACE PEOPLE NEED TO GO.
NORTHERN SUBURB
EASTERN SUBURB
SOUTHERN SUBURB
WESTERN SUBURB
YOU'D DO WELL TO REMEMBER THAT, BECAUSE THE INQUISITION HAS BEEN PRETTY STRICT ABOUT IT AND AREN'T KIND TO THOSE WHO DON'T FOLLOW INSTRUCTIONS.

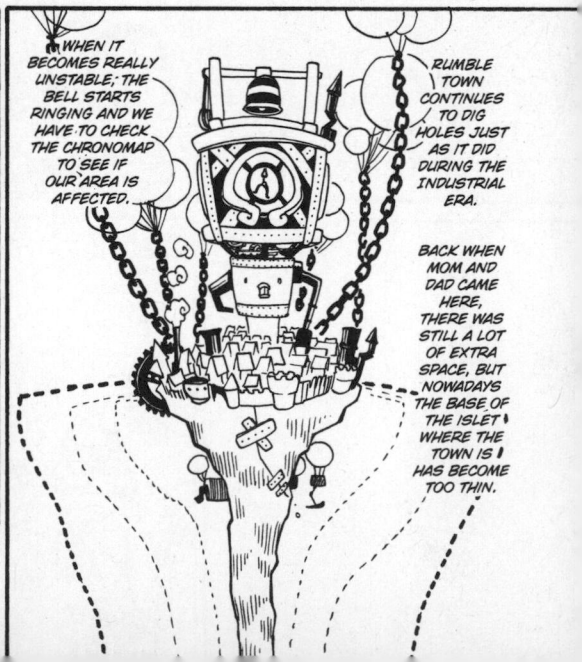
WHEN IT BECOMES REALLY UNSTABLE, THE BELL STARTS RINGING AND WE HAVE TO CHECK THE CHRONOMAP TO SEE IF OUR AREA IS AFFECTED.
RUMBLE TOWN CONTINUES TO DIG HOLES JUST AS IT DID DURING THE INDUSTRIAL ERA.
BACK WHEN MOM AND DAD CAME HERE, THERE WAS STILL A LOT OF EXTRA SPACE, BUT NOWADAYS THE BASE OF THE ISLET WHERE THE TOWN IS HAS BECOME TOO THIN.

BLAH, BLAH, BLAH...
WHO CARES ABOUT YOUR PROBLEMS! I'M HERE FOR THE NEMESIS, NOT FOR YOU TO BORE ME TO DEATH!
DURING THE EVACUATION, WORKERS TRY TO RESTORE BALANCE BY PATCHING UP ANY CRACKS.
AND HERE I THOUGHT YOU GUYS WERE JUST HAVING A GIANT PARTY!
THEY MAY EVEN ADD BALLOONS TO ALLEVIATE OTHER AREAS.
SAME HERE...
EITHER WAY, OUR SON RAN INTO A NEMESIS DURING ONE OF THE EVACUATIONS.
HMPH...
THERE YOU GO, HONEYBUN.
I SWEAR, I'LL STICK MY FOOT UP THE BUTT OF ANYONE WHO DARES TAKE A SWIPE AT MY FAMILY!
WHAT?! WATCH YOUR LANGUAGE, WITCH!
NO MATTER HOW BIG YOUR 'CLIP' SIZE!
CAB SIZE!
WE BELIEVE YOU! WE RAN INTO A PACK OF NEMESES EARLIER.
COME NEAR ME AGAIN, AND I'LL DROPKICK YOU...
WHAT DOES A NEMESIS LOOK LIKE?
HA HA!
DO THEY ALSO SMELL BAD LIKE YOU WIZARDS?
THANK THE HEAVENS, HE SURVIVED. BUT NOW WE KNOW WHAT'S ROAMING THROUGH RUMBLE TOWN AND WE'RE SCARED FOR OUR OTHER KIDS' SAFETY.
DESPITE ALL OF THE DISAPPEARANCES, THE AUTHORITIES WON'T BELIEVE US.

WITHOUT AN OFFICIAL REQUEST, THE BREADTH OF WHAT WE CAN DO IS VERY LIMITED! WE CAN'T INVESTIGATE OR USE MAGIC.
AND DEPENDING ON THE LAWS OF AN ISLET, WE MIGHT NOT EVEN TECHNICALLY BE ALLOWED TO BE HERE AT ALL!
NOT ONLY IS IT DIFFICULT, IT'S TOO DANGEROUS FOR US TO BE WORKING ILLEGALICITY!
HE SMELLS AND SPEAKS BADLY!
HAVE SOME TEA, HONEY-BUN.
AAAH!!
THE PROBLEM IS THAT WE'RE A BIT SHORT ON MANPOWER TO HANDLE THIS AMOUNT OF NEMESES...
SHORT ON MAN-POWER?! I'M IN GREAT SHAPE! I'M AS STRONG AS A DOZEN MEN!
SURE ...
BUT IDEALLY YOUR REQUEST SHOULD ALSO GO THROUGH THE INQUISITION.
ALMA NEVER REALLY BOTHERED WITH ALL THAT PAPERWORK.
THAT ONLY WORKS IN THE MIDDLE OF NOWHERE—IN ALL OF THE POMPO HILLS OF THE WORLD!
TELL THEM WHAT HAPPENED TO YOU.
TAJ
- SON OF THE ZEHD FAMILY -
AH, THERE'S TAJ!
WE WERE JUST TALKING ABOUT YOU. COME SAY HELLO TO THE NICE WIZARDS.

IT'S JUST A COLD, MOM! THAT'S ALL!
AND WHAT ABOUT ALL THAT PURPLE LIQUID RUNNING OUT OF YOUR NOSE AND MOUTH? ARE YOU TELLING ME THAT'S NOT AN *INFECTION*!?
MOM, I ALREADY TOLD YOU I DIDN'T SEE ANYTHING! I MADE A MISTAKE!
I THINK IT WAS JUST A BIG MOLE... OR A DUCK!
SO? IT COULD HAPPEN!
A TEN-METER-LONG DUCK?
I TOLD YOU, IT'S NOTHING! OKAY? SO JUST LEAVE ME ALONE!
I'M OUTTA HERE!
IT STINKS IN HERE!
WAS IT BIG?
WHAT'D IT LOOK LIKE? WHERE'D YA SEE IT?
EHH... IF YOU'RE INFECTED, THEN THAT MEANS YOU CAME INTO CONTACT WITH THE ***SOURCE NEMESIS***. CONTACT WITH ECHOES WON'T KILL ANYONE OR INFECT SURVIVORS.
NOTHING BETTER THAN A GOOD, HOT CUP OF TEA TO EASE TENSION.
BUT YOU'RE OUR GUESTS, SO STAY!
HONEY, MY *LEGS* DON'T NEED ANY MORE TEA...
HE'S NOT WRONG!
THIS MATTER CONCERNS OUR FAMILY AND OUR FAMILY ALONE.

-RUMBLE TOWN-
CENTRAL SUBURB, INQUISITION CAPTAIN'S OFFICE
OH, CAPTAIN! HUFF HUFF!
CAPTAIN!
MAJOR VIL SALVAGE, ARE YOU POSSESSED OR SOMETHING?
N-NO, CAPTAIN!
AN INQUISITOR DOESN'T RUN YELLING THROUGH HALLS. GIVE ME 83 PUSH-UPS!
W-WAIT, 83?!
WOULD YOU RATHER HAVE A ROUND NUMBER?
THEN DROP AND GIVE ME 10,000!!!
THE CAPTAIN REALLY LIKES HIS EXTREMES...
ONE... TWO... THREE...
KONRAD OF MARBOURG
-INQUISITOR CAPTAIN-

NOT EVEN AN OLD PERSON? OR A HANDICAPPED PERSON? GIVE ME AT LEAST A DEAD CAT OR SOMETHING!
NONE, MY CAPTAIN... HUFF!
NO, CAPTAIN... HUFF...THE INCIDENT OCCURRED... HUFF... DURING AN EVACUATION.
HA HA! NOW THAT'S EXCELLENT NEWS!!
A WIZARD!? IN MY TERRITORY?!
HOW MANY DEAD, MAJOR? HOW MANY?!
NOW, MAJOR. YOU HAVE MY ATTENTION, BUT DON'T STOP.
EVIDENCE SUGGESTED... HUFF...THAT... HUFF...FANTASIA HAD A ROLE TO... HUFF...PLAY IN IT...HRGGH...
AN EXPLOSION... HUFF...HAS DESTROYED... HUFF...THE SIDE OF A BUILDING.
MAJOR! BRING ME TO THE SCENE AS SOON AS YOU'RE DONE.
AND ALL OF YOU, MAKE HE SURE HE DOESN'T FORGET TO COUNT! IF HE DOES, LOCK HIM UP FOR INSUBORDINATION.
TOO BAD... IF ONLY THE TOWNSPEOPLE HAD SUFFERED ONE OR TWO LOSSES TO CRY ABOUT, WE COULD'VE HAD OURSELVES A MANHUNT...
I GUESS WE'LL HAVE TO STICK TO AN INVESTI-GATION!
IS IT REALLY TOO MUCH TO ASK FOR JUST A LITTLE BIT OF CLASS?

SLUP
CAPTAIN DRAGUNOV, I WASN'T EXPECTING YOU. I AM SINCERELY GRATEFUL FOR YOUR VISIT.
AREN'T WE LIVING A COZY LIFE! A LARGE CASTLE, IMPOSING FURNITURE, A CELLAR FILLED WITH DELICIOUS WINES...
THE RESULT OF NUMEROUS POLICE RAIDS, I ASSUME ...
SINCERELY GRATEFUL? IS THAT A JOKE, KONRAD?
IT'S CAPTAIN OF MARBOURG.
KONRAD, MY BROTHER!
HEY THERE.

AAH! NOW THERE'S THE KONRAD I KNOW!
HOW DARE YOU!
YOU RUDE, SNOOPING, HALF-WITTED JERK FACE!!
I'M THE BOSS HERE AND THIS IS MY STATION. I HAVE THE DECIDING VOTE! SO SHOW ME SOME RESPECT!
YOU'RE NOT MY BOSS ANYMORE, CAPTAIN DRAGUNOV!
I DON'T DO 12 HOURS OF BODY-BUILDING EVERY DAY–
THEN AGAIN, IF YOU DO 12 HOURS OF BODYBUILDING EVERY DAY...
IS IT ME OR DID YOU GET EVEN BIGGER, RADDIE?!
SLURP
CAPTAIN OF MARBOURG.
IT'S WRITTEN IN YOUR PLANNER, RIGHT?
...
YOU'RE TAKING A SEAT AND I'M GOING TO SHUT UP!!!
OKAY, OKAY, TAKE A SEAT, I'LL SHUT UP.
DON'T TELL ME WHAT TO DO!!
A GROUP? SO MORE THAN ONE WIZARD? HA HA HA!
I WAS JUST ABOUT TO START AN INVESTIGATION INTO THAT FANTASIA EXPLOSION!
OH, NOTHING OFFICIAL. I CAN TELL YOU THAT I'M AFTER A CERTAIN GROUP OF WIZARDS THOUGH.
HMM... WAIT, THAT'S NOT RIGHT...
WHAT ARE YOU DOING HERE? NOBODY TOLD ME YOU WERE COMING.

GO UP JUST TWO MORE!
THE COMMANDER?
THESE AREN'T MY ORDERS– THEY COME FROM HIGHER UP.
WELL, YOU CAN FORGET ABOUT YOUR INVESTIGATION FOR NOW.
!!
DRAGUNOV!! DON'T YOU DARE GIVE ME ANY MORE ORDERS OR I SWEAR I WILL RIP YOUR EYES OUT THROUGH YOUR NOSTRILS!!
I CAN'T SAY. I'M WAITING HERE FOR FURTHER INSTRUCTIONS.
GENERAL TORQUE?!
WHY?
YOU SEEM A LITTLE WOUND UP.
YOU'RE THE ONE WHO'S WOUND UP!!
JUST STAY HERE AND REST. I'LL GO AND TAKE CARE OF THE EXPLOSION.
SHUT UP!!!
CALM DOWN, KONRAD.
YOU CALM DOWN!! AND DON'T TELL ME WHAT TO DO!!
RAAAAH! I'VE GOT WIZARDS WALKING AROUND MY CITY AND I'M SUPPOSED TO JUST STAY HERE AND DO NOTHING?!
AND WITHOUT BEING TOLD WHY?!
YOU'RE GOING TO STAY HERE AND REST WHILE I GO TAKE CARE OF THE EXPLOSION!!!

BAM
HFF.!! 231!
HFF.!! 232!
HFF!! 233!
SLURP
SLURP
WHAT THE HELL JUST HAPPENED?!

?
AAAH...

I LOOKED OVER THERE AND SUDDENLY GOT HIT BY SOME BAD VERTIGISM...
VERTIGEE?
ARE YOU ALL RIGHT?
YOU MEAN LIKE THIS MORNING WITH THE NEMESIS?

ME TOO, BUT NOT TO THE POINT OF GETTING SICK! DOC, YOU MUST BE HYPERSENSITIVE TO FANTASIA!
PSH, YEAH RIGHT! I JUST HAVE A GOOD SENSE FOR TROUBLE! AND THAT ABANDONED BUILDING HAS TROUBLE WRITTEN ALL OVER IT!
YEAH... HOW'D YOU KNOW ABOUT THAT?
I FEEL A LOT OF FANTASIA CONCENTRATED OVER THERE.

TAJ SAID HE SAW THE NEMESIS AROUND HERE.
THAT WAS WEEKS AGO. WE'D BE LUCKY IF THERE'S EVEN A TRACE OF IT LEFT.
WHY AM I HERE TOO?
THE TOILET PAPER MAN IS AFTER YOU. IT'S SAFER IF WE'RE ALL TOGETHER.

SO THERE WAS A NEMESIS HIDING IN HERE!
WUNCH

A TEN-METER-LONG DUCK...

CHAPTER 9

A THEATER PIECE

THIS IS PROOF THAT A SOURCE NEMESIS USED TO LIVE HERE!
ALMA'S SHOWN ME A FEW BEFORE, BUT NEVER ONE *THAT* BIG!
SEE! I TOLD YOU THIS PLACE WAS TROUBLE!
NEMESES MOVE AROUND TOO MUCH, SO THE TREES DON'T HAVE TIME TO GROW THIS LARGE.
YOU CAN USUALLY FIND A NUMBER OF THEM IN AREAS WHERE A NEMESIS LIVES.
THAT'S A *FEATHER TREE!!*

BUT TAKE A LOOK AT THE AMOUNT OF FEATHERS IT HAS AND HOW BIG IT IS!
THE SOURCE NEMESIS MUST HAVE SPENT DAYS IN THIS PLACE.
THIS BUILDING MUST HAVE SERVED AS SOME KIND OF NEST.

THERE'S A LARGE SLIDING SHUTTER UP THERE.
AND YOU'RE SAYING THE NEMESES OPENED AND CLOSED IT USING THEIR LITTLE FINGERS?
THAT WOULD BE QUITE UNUSUAL, YES...

BUT HOW'D A SOURCE NEMESIS AND ALL THOSE ECHOES STAY HERE IN THE MIDDLE OF THE TOWN WITHOUT BEING DISCOVERED? IN INCOGNINITY!
THE WINDOWS AND ENTRANCES ARE BOARDED UP—IT'S THE PERFECT HIDING SPOT!
THEN HOW'D THEY GET IN AND OUT?
INCOGNITUDE? DISCRETIOUSNESS?

DONG
DONG
!!

THAT WOULDN'T EVEN BE THE WEIRDEST THING ABOUT THIS. I MEAN, A HERD OF MONSTERS ENTERING AND EXITING A BUILDING COULDN'T STAY UNNOTICED FOR THAT LONG!

DONG
HEAD TO THE SOUTH SUBURB! FASTER!
COME ON! FASTER!
DONG
KEEP UP THE PACE!
ANYONE CAUGHT NOT EVACUATING WILL FACE 15 YEARS IN PRISON!
THIS IS TO ENSURE EVERYONE'S SAFTEY!
WILL YOU HIDE ALREADY, YOU IDIOT!
DONG
DONG
THEY'RE EVACUATING THE AREA!
NO, WE'RE STAYING HERE.
WE'D ALSO BETTER MOVE ALONG BEFORE THEY CATCH US. OR WORSE, BEFORE THE ENTIRE AREA COLLAPSES!
AND WHILE THE INQUISITION IS LOOKING FOR US TOO!
GET OUR BUTTS HANDED TO US BY 100 NEMESES WHILE A MURDEROUS WALKING TOILET-PAPER ROLL IS AFTER US...
...ALL WHILE THIS AREA COULD COLLAPSE AT ANY TIME!!
A HUNDRED? BARELY...
IT'S LIKE 15 AT MOST.
IF WE STAY AROUND HERE AND KEEP OUR EYES OPEN, MAYBE WE'LL HAVE A CHANCE TO–
WE ARRIVED HERE IN THE MIDDLE OF AN EVACUATION AND ENCOUNTERED THE NEMESES. TAJ ALSO MENTIONED SEEING THE SOURCE NEMESIS WHILE EVACUATING.
THEY ONLY MOVE DURING EVACUATIONS!

GET DOWN HERE IMMEDIATELY!
THAT BUILDING BELONGS TO THE INQUISITION!!
MÉLIE, YOUR BROOM!
ACK!!
HEY, YOU UP THERE! THE GUY SCREAMING !!
I DON'T SEE HIM ANYMORE.
HE'S GONE?
IF YOU DON'T EVACUATE THE AREA THIS INSTANT, WE-
DONG
DONG
DONG
HE JUST DISAP-PEARED!
I FEEL LIKE I SAW HIM FLY AWAY...
BLEURP
FLY AWAY? HA HA HA!
THAT'S A BIRD, DUH!
HE JUST THREW UP ON ME!
SPLOOSH
BIRDS GET SICK. IT HAPPENS.

THERE ARE SO MANY OF THEM!
THERE'S MORE THAN 15, IT SEEMS.
THERE THEY ARE!
DONG
DONG
DONG
DONG
DOC WAS RIGHT, WE ARE SHORT ON MANPOWER!
WAIT A SEC, THEY'RE SPREADING OUT...
?
...
SETH?
YOU'RE A TRAPPER, RIGHT? YOU MUST HAVE SOMETHING THAT CAN CATCH THEM, RIGHT? AND THERE'S ONLY THREE OF THEM.
THERE! A SMALL GROUP OF THEM IS HEADED THIS WAY!
OKAY, HOLD THIS.
SURE.
WE'D HAVE TO KEEP THEM WITHIN THIS SMALL AREA, AND EVEN THEN I'M NOT SURE IF–

BOP
BOP
METEOR DROPS!
FSHH
SHHH
FSHHH
BRAM
BRAM
BRAM
FSHHH
FSHHH

TITAN PUNCH!!
!!
BLAAAARGHHH...
BROOOO!!

HFF
HFFF
AND THAT OTHER ONE IS BARELY BREATHING.
THAT ONE IS STUCK UNDER DEBRIS.
THIS ONE LOOKS STUNNED.
MÉLIE SHOULD BE ABLE TO TRAP THEM.
VROOO
BIOP
BIOP
METEOR DROPS!
WSHHHF
FFFFFFFFFF
VIIIIIII...

FSHH
GRU
IT'S COMING BACK AT ME?!

WHAT'RE YOU DOING? IT'S GETTING AWAY!!
I HURT MYSELF MORE BY KICKING MYSELF IN THE NOSE THIS MORNING!
NO, NOT GOOD! YAGA WAS RIGHT! I JUST GOT HIT BY MY OWN ATTACK AND I BARELY GAVE MYSELF A NOSEBLEED!
YOU KICKED YOURSELF IN THE NOSE?
WHAT? YOU'D RATHER HAVE A BROKEN ARM?!
DO YOU HIT YOURSELF OFTEN?
WELL, AT LEAST A RIB...
SETH ?!
OH, GOOD!
SETH?
...
THE PROBLEM IS THAT THE NEMESIS WILL THROW A WIND ATTACK AS SOON AS IT SEES US. MR. SETH, CAN YOU...
I WILL NEED TO GET CLOSE TO THEM FOR A FEW SECONDS IF I WANT TO STOP THEM.
VROOOOO...

MÉLIE! I CAN'T HOLD THIS FOREVER!!

SHHHHHHHHH
FSHHHH
SWF
SETH!! GET OUT OF THE CIRCLE!!
?!

GRAVEM CARCEREM— ETCH PRISON!!
NOW!
VWSH

ω-
...ω
BUT THIS IS TOO MUCH!
HERE, SHORT RECKONINGS MAKE LONG FRIENDS!
THAT MAKES US SUPER GOOD FRIENDS!
OKAY! OKAY!!
NOW YOU CAN PAY ME BACK FAST!!
NOW YOU HAVE TO HELP ME, DOC!
ONE OF THEM IS HALF-DEAD, BUT...
AH, RIGHT!
DID WE JUST CAPTURE THREE NEMESES ALIVE?!
DID...
THREE? OH, MY BRAVE ADVENTURIST!
LET'S GET MARRIED THREE TIMES!
LET'S MAKE THREE KIDS!
LET'S BUY THREE HOUSES!

NOW THAT THE HARD PART IS OVER...
YOU'RE NOT DONE?
HA HA HA! WE'LL MAKE SO MUCH MONEY!
NO MORE GRASS AND DIRT FOR MEALS!
AND I CAN FINALLY GET MY OWN PLACE! AND BUY A BROOM! AND...
PAY ME BACK!!
YES MA'AM!!
I COMBINED THE BARRIER WITH A BONDING SPELL. ON THE GROUND, THEIR MOVEMENTS BECOME A LOT HEAVIER, AND SINCE THEY CAN'T FLY...
WHAT IF THEY JUMP OVER YOUR BARRIER?
I TRIED IT OUT ALREADY ON LIVE SPECIMENS BACK AT THE ARTEMIS INSTITUTE. IT TAKES QUITE A LOT OF ENERGY TO DO!
I STILL HAVE TO SEAL THEM ON THE PARCHMENTS OVER THERE.
+1
?
MÉLIE, THE PRECOGNISTA!
WHO KNEW YOU WERE SO TALENTED, MÉLIE?!
...
HURRAY FOR MÉLIE!
HURRAY FOR MÉLIE!

...TO HELP YOU FIND RADIANT!
WE'LL DO EVERY-THING WE CAN...
FRIENDS FOR LIFE (^0^)
THEY LOOK LIKE SUCH SUPER FRIENDS!
I WANT ONE!
DOC CASTLE
PWIII
WOOOOH!
YEAAAAH!
HA HA HA!
THERE'S FOUR... FIVE... SIX...SEVEN! THAT'S A TOTAL OF SEVEN NEMESES WE'VE NOW CAUGHT!!
+1
+1
LOOK, THERE'S EVEN MORE NEMESES FALLING DOWN!!
WHAT'S GOING ON?!
THEY MUST HAVE BEEN ALERTED BY THE DISTRESS CALL OF THEIR TRAPPED BUDDIES!
+1
TCHAK
TCHAK
WHIZZZZ

BLORPS
SPLORCH
IT... IT'S RAINING VOMIT.
MOM, DAD...
HAH HAH! RUMBLE TOWN! WE'LL BE LIVING IT UP HERE, YOU'LL SEE! WE'RE GOING TO BUILD A NEW STORE! I CAN ALREADY IMAGINE IT...

Chapter 10
Domitor

WE MEET AGAIN, HORN-HEAD.
NOOOO!! HE TOOK THEM ALL!!
MY FRIENDS !!
PWIII!
MY WIFE! MY KIDS!! YOU KILLED 'EM!!
VENEFICIUM REVELARE-MAGIC REVEAL!
LET'S SEE...
GRIMM WOULD LIKE TO APOLO-GIZE FOR RUINING YOUR PLANS.
A BARRIER, A BINDING SPELL AND CONTAIN-MENT PARCH-MENTS...
WELL, WELL... LOOKS LIKE YOU WERE HOPING TO CAPTURE THESE NEMESES.
THAT'S HIM?!
I'M GOING TO KICK YOUR BUTT, TOILET-PAPER FACE!!
THAT'S A MUMMY, NOT TOILET PAPER!!

ALL THESE DISAPPEARANCES NECESSITATE CERTAIN SOMEWHAT COMPLEX LOGISTICS, YOU SEE.
NOW PLEASE EXCUSE GRIMM, BUT A NUMBER OF POOR LOST SOULS OUTSIDE ARE IN NEED OF GRIMM'S ATTENTION.
MÉLIE, THE BARRIER! HE'S ESCAPING!!
FARE-WELL.

I MARKED HIM!
IT'S FINE, AT LEAST HE CAN'T SNEAK UP ON US ANYMORE ...
AAAAH!! HE GOT AWAY!

HOW'D YOU DO THAT?
THIS IS THE FIRST TIME I'VE USED IT ON A WIZARD. I'M TIRED!
I DON'T GET IT.
IT'S TOO MUCH... TOO MANY NEMESES AND NOT DEAD ENOUGH...

THANKS TO THAT MARK, THERE WON'T BE ANY MORE NASTY SURPRISES– I'LL BE ABLE TO SENSE IT WHEN HE'S CLOSE...
I USUALLY USE IT TO ANTICIPATE A NEMESIS'S MOVEMENTS AND SET UP TRAPS FOR IT.

...AND HE WAS EVEN BRAGGING ABOUT MAKING PEOPLE DISAPPEAR.
I JUST WONDER WHAT HIS DEAL IS. HE'S AFTER THE NEMESES AND US...
A CRYING ANT? YOU MAKE NO SENSE...
YOU MEAN MISCREANT?
I THINK HE'S JUST A MISCRIER!
THAT WAY, WE CAN USE A CLAIRVOYANCE SPELL IF WE EVER NEED TO TRACK HIM. BUT THE PROBLEM IS THAT HE MIGHT SENSE THE FANTASIA BEING ACTIVATED ...
A SEAL WOULD HAVE BEEN BETTER, BUT I DIDN'T HAVE ENOUGH TIME FOR THAT.
AND IN THE WORST CASE, HE MIGHT USE IT TO FIND US FIRST.
WHEN I KNEW WE WOULDN'T BE ABLE TO STOP HIM, I ATTACHED AN INFINITESIMAL AMOUNT OF FANTASIA TO HIM.
COMING BACK WITH ONE OR EVEN A THOUSAND NEMESES WON'T CHANGE ANY OF THAT!
IT'S NOT LIKE I HAVE THE GUTS TO MAKE THE FIRST MOVE ANYWAY!
I'M A COWARD... EVERYONE KNOWS IT.
WHAT ABOUT YOUR PROMISE?! YOU TOLD THAT WAITRESS THAT YOU'D—
TOO BAD!
IT'S TOO MUCH TROUBLE... THE STRESS IS MAKING ME SICK! I'VE GOT COLD SWEETS, VERTIGEEZ AND CAN'T EAT.
SHOWER AND SLEEP!
I'M LEAVING FOR THE ARTEMIS INSTITUTE FIRST THING TOMORROW! JUST CALL ME WHEN YOU'RE DONE.
IT'LL MAKE MORE SENSE AFTER A GOOD NIGHT'S REST.
YEAH, IT'LL CLEAR YOUR HEAD...

I DO HOPE YOU'LL EXCUSE GRIMM FOR THIS SLIGHTLY UNCOMFORTABLE MODE OF TRANSPORTATION.
GNNN!
GNN!
BUT REST ASSURED, THIS IS WHERE THIS TRIP ENDS FOR YOU.

OH, THERE'S A LOT OF YOU HERE TONIGHT TO WELCOME OUR NEW GUESTS!
PLEASE, DO TAKE GOOD CARE OF THESE TWO NEW BRAVE SOULS.
WUSH
HMFF!! HMMMM!!
DON'T FORGET TO CLOSE UP AND DON'T DRAW ATTENTION ...
...AND BE SURE TO TREAT THEM WITH THE SAME RESPECT GRIMM SHOWED YOU.

DON'T GET SO WORKED UP. I HAVEN'T EVEN SAID ANYTHING YET!
OH, PLEASE! NO MORE QUESTIONS ABOUT RADIANT, I'VE HAD IT UP TO HERE WITH THAT!
YOU'VE BEEN STUDYING NEMESES FOR A WHILE NOW, RIGHT?

DOC!
SRNK... ZZZ...
HEY, DOC!
SRNNNK... ZZZZZ...
DOC, YOU ASLEEP?
CAN'T YOU HEAR!! SRNNK ZZZ! SRNNK ZZZ!!

EARLIER, WHEN I WAS HOLDING DOWN THE NEMESIS, I NOTICED SOMETHING ...
IT HAD A VERY SMALL MARK ON IT. LIKE A SYMBOL.

THE ONLY THING THEY HAD IN COMMON WAS THAT THEY BOTH HAD WHITE SHELLS ON THEIR HEADS.
TAKE THIS ONE, FOR EXAMPLE. I FOUND THIS ONE ON A NEMESIS THAT WOULD SPIT MAGMA AND ONE THAT TURNED WATER INTO POISON.
Protection
Lava vomit (part)
Over there
Non-toxic trail
13/10
Freak-out-meter MAX
Toxic stinger
Under the eye
Symbol #23
White protector hull
Sensitive to magma
Tentacles with toxic tips
Freak-out-meter MAX
15/10
EVERY NEMESIS HAS A MARK ON THEM, BUT NOBODY KNOWS WHAT THEY MEAN.

DID IT RESEMBLE ANY OF THESE?
YEAH, EXACTLY! WHAT IS IT?
I CAN'T SAY FOR SURE, BUT I'VE SEEN ABOUT 50 OF THEM.
SOMETIMES I'LL FIND THE SAME SYMBOLS ON DIFFERENT NEMESES. I'VE TRIED TO ESTABLISH A CLASSIFICATION METHOD, BUT THEY DON'T SEEM TO BE FOLLOWING ANY KIND OF LOGIC.

HA... HMM...
HUH?
PLEASE TELL ME...
...IT WASN'T GLOWING, RIGHT?
IF YOU SEE THE MARK GLOWING THEN THAT MEANS THAT THE SOURCE NEMESIS AND ECHOES ARE BEING CONTROLLED BY SOMEONE.
THE ONLY THING WE DO KNOW IS THAT WHEN THE SYMBOL IS LIT UP, THAT MEANS THE NEMESIS IS BEING CONTROLLED BY A TAMER WIZARD-A DOMITOR.
THAT WOULD BE THE WORST POSSIBLE SITUATION EVER... HA HA!!

THEY'VE RETURNED.
WE LOST A LOT OF THEM TODAY, BUT...
...IT'LL ALL BE OVER SOON, I PROMISE.
IT'LL ALL BE OVER SOON...

AND THE ROOF OF THE THEATER COLLAPSED, CAUSING SEVERAL THOUSANDS IN MATERIAL DAMAGES!
HEAR YE, HEAR YE! ACCORDING TO A NEW IMMIGRATION SURVEY, 72 PERCENT OF RESIDENTS REPORT FEELING UNEASY WITH THE INCREASING NUMBER OF FOREIGNERS, WHILE UNEMPLOYMENT IS ON THE RISE...
FREE WANDERING OBSERVER'S EXPOSÉ
DANG
DONG
YES, I DO FEEL UNEASY!
VERY UNEASY!
HEAR YE, HEAR YE! IN CONJUNCTION, THE SILENT VISIT OF CAPTAIN DART DRAGUNOV FUELS ANOTHER RUMOR–ARE WIZARDS HIDING IN RUMBLE TOWN? ARE THEY LINKED TO THE IMMIGRANT RINGS? WHO KNOWS?!
...AND 53 PERCENT SAY THEY ARE IN FAVOR OF MASS DEPORTATION OF IMMIGRANTS TO THEIR HOME ISLETS.
WHAT? WIZARDS? WHERE?!
ARE YOU HIDING THEM?
GO BACK TO YOUR HOME ISLET NOW!
HEY! I WAS BORN HERE!
HEAR YE, HEAR YE! INQUISITOR CAPTAIN KONRAD OF MARBOURG STRONGLY CONDEMNS THIS BELLIGERENT ACT IN RUMBLE TOWN.
THE POPULATION FEARS AN INCREASE IN POWER OF THE ILLEGAL IMMIGRANT RING'S DESTRUCTIVE BEHAVIOR THROUGH SYMBOLIC TERRORISTIC ACTS THAT LAY WASTE TO OUR FREEDOM OF EXPRESSION. THIS ATMOSPHERE IS UNFORTUNATELY REMINISCENT OF THE TIME SHORTLY PRECEDING THE EVENTS LEADING TO THE COLLAPSE OF THE NORTHEASTERN SUBURB 15 YEARS AGO.

CLAP
CLAP
HOT WINDS FROM THE SOUTH ARE SAID TO BE THE CAUSE OF THE METEOROLOGICAL RAMPAGE.
AGAIN?! EVEN THEIR WINDS ARE INFESTING OUR LIVES!
HEAR YE, HEAR YE! WITHOUT FURTHER DELAY, THE WEATHER REPORT– VIOLENT TORNADOES HAVE YET AGAIN STRUCK OUR ISLET LAST NIGHT, RESULTING IN WEAKENING PARTS OF THE NORTHERN SUBURB'S INFRASTRUCTURE.
BRAVO, KONRAD.
THE RUMORS ABOUT THE WIZARDS... YOU'RE THE ONE WHO FED THEM TO THE MEDIA, RIGHT?
WHAT ARE YOU TALKING ABOUT, CAPTAIN DRAGUNOV?
JUST ONE LITTLE SPARK AND RUMBLE TOWN WILL GO DOWN IN FLAMES, JUST LIKE IT DID 15 YEARS AGO.
BUT, JUST LIKE THEN, THEY WON'T SUCCEED IN HUNTING THE INFECTED...
THEIR FEAR, THEIR ANGER... YOU'RE STIRRING THE POT SO THEY'LL INSIST ON A MANHUNT ON THEIR OWN.
SMART THINKING... YOUR HANDS ARE TIED, SO YOU'RE MAKING SURE THAT THE PEOPLE WILL TAKE CARE OF THE PROBLEM FOR YOU.

STRANGE MEN AND WOMEN JUST WANDERING AROUND...THEY'RE EVERYWHERE! IN SOME PLACES YOU CAN'T FIND A SINGLE NORMAL PERSON TO SAVE YOUR LIFE!
SO? BURNING DOWN PARTS OF THE DUMP THAT RUMBLE TOWN HAS BECOME WOULDN'T BE SO BAD! HAVE YOU SEEN THE STATE OF THE NORTHERN SUBURB? IT'S COMPLETELY RUN-DOWN!
OH, THAT'S A WONDERFUL IDEA! LET'S BOIL THE FOREIGNER CHILDREN AND SERVE THEM IN A MEAT STEW FOR THE ALIENS!
THESE FIENDS IMPOSE THEIR LIFESTYLES ON US. SHOULD WE JUST ACCEPT IT?
YOU KNOW WHAT I MEANT! STOP ACTING SO SMUG, DRAGUNOV!
IF ALIENS APPEARED TOMORROW AND WANTED TO EAT OUR CHILDREN, WOULD WE LET THEM OUT OF RESPECT FOR THEIR CULTURE?
WANT TO KNOW WHAT I THINK? A HELMET AND A SIX-INCH-LONG MUSTACHE IS WHAT A REAL MAN LOOKS LIKE!
TRUE, TRUE. THEY WON'T EVEN MAKE AN EFFORT TO BLEND IN AT ALL!
ENOUGH WITH THE JOKES!
THEY NEED TO LEAVE.
NOT TO MENTION WE'RE ALREADY OVERPOPULATED! THERE'S NOT ENOUGH WORK TO GO AROUND.
DRAGUNOV, SOMETIMES I WONDER WHOSE SIDE YOU'RE REALLY ON!
MY MAIN CONCERN IS TO SAFEGUARD THE PEACE AND MORAL INTEGRITY OF RUMBLE TO–
ANY THREAT, WHETHER IT BE FROM THE INSIDE OR THE OUTSIDE, MUST BE ERADICATED!
SO THE WIZARDS ARE JUST AN EXCUSE.
IT'S THE IMMIGRANTS YOU'RE REALLY AFTER.

YOU'VE BEEN SNOOPING AROUND AGAIN!
YOU HEARD ME. THE RECORDS RELATED TO THE NORTHERN SUBURB ARE *FILLED* WITH COMPLAINTS. MYSTERIOUS DISAPPEARANCES, NEMESIS SIGHTINGS...
WHAT?!
YEAH, YEAH. *BLAH, BLAH, BLAH...* SAVE YOUR SPEECH FOR THE CITIZENS, WILL YA? I'M NOT BUYING IT.
YOU'RE LETTING A NEMESIS WANDER AROUND.
KONRAD, SOMETIMES I WONDER WHOSE SIDE *YOU'RE* REALLY ON, BUT...
CONSIDERING THE POTENTIAL THREAT THESE WIZARDS REPRESENT, WE WILL CONDUCT OUR INVESTIGATION AS DICTATED IN THAT REPORT.
FOR THE SAME REASON I'M HERE.
THE MIRACLE WORKERS?! WHY?
TORQUE AND A COUPLE OF HIS THAUMATURGES ARE COMING TO RUMBLE TOWN *TOMORROW*.
...WE'RE OLD FRIENDS, SO LET ME LEAVE YOU THIS ONE PIECE OF ADVICE—GET YOUR HOUSE BACK IN ORDER, FAST.

SO CHEER UP, KONRAD. IT'S HUNTING SEASON!

THE WIZARDS!
I KNEW WE SHOULDN'T HAVE DONE THIS!!
WHERE'RE THE WIZARDS?!

AAAH !!
HAVE SOME TEA!
CALM DOWN, HONEY-BUN.
SHHH

IF THEY FIND YOU, WE'RE ALL DONE FOR!
THE INQUISITION HAS STARTED AN INVESTIGATION! THE HUNT FOR WIZARDS HAS OFFICIALLY STARTED!

WHATSHUP FNOW?
YOU'RE STILL HERE?!
LEAVE! YOU'RE PUTTING MY FAMILY IN DANGER!

WIZARD AND FOREIGNERS
IT'S HIGH TIME!
THEY'RE LOOKING FOR INFECTED ONES AND ARE ALSO ATTACKING FOREIGNERS.
THEY'RE GOING AFTER EVERYONE!
DAD! YOU'RE BLEEDING!!
I'M ALL RIGHT.
BUT NONE OF YOU LEAVE THE HOUSE, GOT IT?
A GROUP OF ARMED CIVILIANS IS TEARING APART THE NEIGHBORHOOD.
WHERE'S DOC?!
HE LEFT EARLY THIS MORNING TO HEAD BACK TO ARTEMIS!
GAAAAH! I KNEW I SHOULDN'T HAVE LET THESE TWO GET INVOLVED IN OUR FAMILY'S BUSINESS!! AND TAJ BEING OUT THERE WITH ALL THE CRAZIES...
DON'T LEAVE– THERE'S INQUISITORS COMING UP THE STAIRS! THEY'RE RANSACKING APARTMENTS!
I'LL GET HIM BACK, SNOOKUMS, PROMISE! HE'S GONNA GET IT LATER!!
HONEY BUN! TAJ ISN'T HERE!
WHAAAT?! THAT RASCAL!
...
WE NEED TO DO SOMETHING!

SO WHAT?
WE'RE HERE FOR THE NEMESES. YOUR FAMILY'S PROBLEMS HAVE NOTHING TO DO–
DON'T YOU DARE GO THROUGH THAT DOOR! OR ELSE!!
WE'RE LEAVING. MÉLIE, YOUR BROOM!
BUT...
WHAT'RE YOU DOING?! THEY'LL BE HERE ANY SECOND!
WE'RE ALL GOING TO END UP IN JAIL BECAUSE OF YOU!! NOW HIDE, YOU FOOL!
GAAAH!!
OR ELSE WHAT?
BROOOOO
?!

SURE I WILL, POPEYE!!
THERE'S MORE WHERE THAT CAME FROM!
YOU'RE GOING TO REGRET ASSAULTING MY DAUGHTER, YOU SCOUNDREL!!
IT'S THE WIZARDS!
YOU'LL SEE! WE'LL FIND THAT SON OF YOURS AND TAKE GOOD CARE OF HIM...
MARK MY WORDS!
DID THEY ATTACK YOU?!
DON'T WORRY, THE INQUISITION WILL DEFEND YOU!
HURRY, AFTER THEM!

JUST ANOTHER REGULAR NIGHT AT THE TOWN CRIER'S HOUSE...

CHAPTER 11

TWO LOOGIES AND SOME PEE

YOU DON'T LOOK SO GOOD.
NO, NO! I'M GOOD.
MY FACE IS DEFINITELY NOT SMASHED...

WAS THERE NOT A BETTER WAY TO HANDLE THE SITUATION?
SURE, BUT...
THE INQUISITION'S PROTECTING THEM, SO NOBODY'LL SUSPECT THEM...
AND WE'RE FREE TO GO AS WELL!

OVER HERE! I GOT ONE!
AAAH!

THAT DOESN'T ALWAYS STOP THEM, TRUST ME!
HE'S JUST A CHILD!
IF WE CAN'T FIND TAJ BEFORE THE MOB DOES, THEN I DON'T EVEN WANT TO IMAGINE WHAT THEY'LL DO TO HIM.

A FILTHY INFECTED ONE!!

BAM
SAME THING! YOU'RE ALL IN IT TOGETHER ANYWAY! YOU BROUGHT 'EM WITH YA'!
A NEMESIS DID THAT! AND ALMA'S HUNTING IT!
AAAH... HE BLED ON MY GLOVE! GOTTA THROW IT AWAY NOW...
MIGHT AS WELL THROW AWAY ALL TH'OTHER FRUIT! YOU SPOILED THEM THE SAME WAY YOU DID THE COWS!
I TOLD YOU, I BOUGHT THEM!
LOOK AT DIS!
WOW, WHAT'S THAT?
MY UNCLE WORKS FOR THE INQUISITION, HE GAVE ME THIS!
YOU'RE ALL WRONG! IT'S BECAUSE THEY LET 'EM TAKE OVER THEIR BODY TO STEAL THEIR SOUL.
WE HAVE TO STAB HIM ALL OVER! IF HE CAN'T FEEL IT ANYMORE, IT MEANS WE FOUND THE SPOT THE DEMON CAME THROUGH!
MY UNCLE SAYS YOU NEED TO FIND THE DEMON'S MARK ...
MY MOMMY SAYS THAT IF PEOPLE DON'T DIE AFTER TOUCHING ONE, IT'S BECAUSE THEIR SIAMESE CATS ARE DREAMING.
A DEMON.
WHAT'S THAT, A NENESIS?
NOOO, IT'S SIGNED A PACT WITH DEMONS!

DON'T MOVE!
STOP IT!!
COME ON, WHERE'S YOUR MARK?
HOLD 'IM TIGHT! HE'S HURTING ME!
STOOOOP!!
IT HURTS!!
TRY HERE!
AAAAH!
FSHH
LEAVE ME ALONE...
SNIFF...
HUFF...
SNIFF...
IT HURTS...
GNNN...
SSSTT

HUFF, HUFF!
SNIFF!
LEAVE ME ALONE...
SNIFF... PLEASE LEAVE...
AAAH...
MY BABIES !!
HNNN...
HRRR ...
HE'S GOT A KNIFE!
FOR GOODNESS SAKE, WHY?!
NOOOWWY...
SO WHY? WHY WOULD YOU DO THIS TO OUR CHILDREN?!
WE LET YOU STAY ON THE ISLET, WE LEAVE YOU ALONE...
YOU'RE A MON-STER!!

BUT... HE'S SO YOUNG...
ARE YOU SURE WE SHOULDN'T WAIT FOR THE INQUISITOR?
FIRST THE EPIDEMIC THAT WIPES OUT HALF OF OUR LIVESTOCK, THEN THIS SNOW THAT JEOPARDIZES OUR FOOD SUPPLIES... AND NOW OUR KIDS ALMOST DIED!!
HE WON'T BE HERE FOR ANOTHER COUPLE OF DAYS, AND WHO KNOWS HOW MANY MORE ATROCITIES THIS LITTLE DEVIL WILL COMMIT BY THEN?!
LOOK AT HIS EYES... I BET HE PUT A HEX ON US!
WE'RE CURSED!
WHAT ELSE DO YOU NEED TO UNDERSTAND?! THE HEAVENS ARE PUNISHING US FOR HAVING TOLERATED WIZARDS ON OUR ISLET!
WE SHOULD KILL IT NOW! AS LONG AS IT STAYS ALIVE, WE'RE PUTTING OURSELVES IN GRAVE DANGER!
THAT WAS A WITCH'S SPIT!
?!
WHAT THE...?
ANYONE ELSE WANT A LOOGIE?
NOW YOU TWO ARE ALSO INFECTED!

WE WON'T BE INTIMIDATED BY THE LIKES OF YOU!
LEAVE, WITCH! OR WE'LL BURN YOU ALONG WITH HIM!
SHE'S LYING, THEIR INFECTIONS AREN'T TRANSMITTABLE!
STOP!
AAAAH!
SOMEBODY HELP!
IT BURNS!
ONLY NEMESES CAN CAUSE AN INFECTION!
OOOH, YOU CAN TRY...
...BUT THEN I'LL HAVE AN EXCUSE TO SLAUGHTER ALL OF YOU!
TSK... MORONS!
TO BE THIS SCARED OF A LITTLE KID... WHAT IN THE WORLD IS THE INQUISITION FEEDING THOSE MINDLESS SHEEP?

NO...
SNIFF!
SNIFF!
ARE YOU OKAY, SETH?
LOOK, THIS ALWAYS HAPPENS. WHENEVER THEY'RE IN TROUBLE, INSTEAD OF FIXING IT THEY LOOK FOR A BAD GUY.
THAT'S WHAT I'M HERE FOR.
DON'T BE THAT PERSON FOR THEM.
...
WHERE DID THEY HURT YOU?
AND WHAT? YOU'LL BECOME THE MONSTER THEY THINK YOU ARE? IS THAT YOUR PLAN?!
EFFERY-WHERE... SNIFF...
ALMA, WHEN I BECOME STRONG LIKE YOU, I'LL COME BACK... SNIFF... AND...
IF YOU DO, I'LL BE THE ONE TO BURN YOU, NITWIT.

I ADMIT IT'S IN NEED OF SOME SPRUCING UP, BUT THAT'S ALL WE COULD AFFORD!
SNIFF... IT LOOKS LAME...
SNIFF... WHAT IS IT?
AN AIRSHIP. I JUST BOUGHT IT! NOW WE CAN STOP MOVING FROM ISLET TO ISLET EVERY TWO WEEKS...
HEY, YOU WANT TO SEE SOMETHING FUN?
STOP CRYING FOR A SECOND AND LOOK UP.
BUT AT LEAST THERE, YOU WON'T HAVE ANYTHING TO WORRY ABOUT– EVEN WHEN I'M OUT HUNTING!
WE'LL BE SAFE UP THERE, YOU'LL SEE.
AND NOBODY ELSE BUT THE BIRDS WILL BOTHER US.
HNFF!!
I DIDN'T DO ANY-THING!

FSSSHHHHHH

HUFF!
HUFF!
PLEEASSE...
WIZARD!
PHEWW, THAT SMELL!

THIS RAIN IS WEIRD... SNIFF SNIFF... IT SMELLS!
RAIN! THE TORCH WENT OUT!

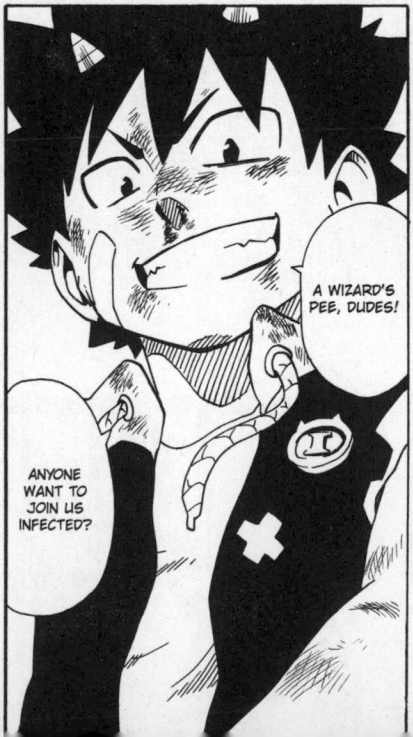
A WIZARD'S PEE, DUDES!
ANYONE WANT TO JOIN US INFECTED?

HEY, UP THERE!
WAIT... THIS ISN'T RAIN, IT'S...
THEY'RE WIZARDS !!

PLEASE PUT IT BAAACK!
WAAAH! STOP MESSING AROUND MÉLIE! OPEN YOUR EYES!
OKAY, OKAY!
I SWALLOWED SOME!! GRAH!
IT'S INFECTED PEE!
WE'RE ALL GONNA DIE!!
TSSS
GREAT...
ARM THE CANNONS! AIM THEM NORTH!
WIZARDS ARE FLYING OVER THE NORTH GATE, CAPTAIN!
BUT THE NORTHERN SUBURB IS FULL OF CIVILIANS, CAPTAIN!
A-AND ONE OF THEM IS PROVOKING US WITH HIS WIENER!
LET'S NOT WASTE TIME ON DETAILS LIKE THAT.
THE MANHUNT COMES FIRST!

SNIFF... ONE OF THEM KNOWS WHERE I LIVE...
THEY'RE GONNA GO AFTER MY FAMILY... THEY THINK WE'RE ALL WIZARDS!
IT'S MY FAULT...
ANYTHING BROKEN?
SNIFF... I DON'T THINK SO...
PLAMY
A BROOM ?!
YOU DON'T HAVE TO BE AFRAID– TRUST US!
NOW LET'S QUICKLY GET ON MÉLIE'S BROOM BEFORE MORE OF THEM COME OVER.
DON'T WORRY! THEY'RE SAFE! THE INQUISITION'S PROTECTING THEM!
AAAAH! THAT HURT!
THERE'S NO WAY THAT SNOT-NOSED BRAT IS GETTING ON MY BROOM.
NOPE. I'LL LEAVE BOOBRIE WITH YOU...

WE'RE OFF!!
THEY'RE UP THERE!
?!
THAT'S THEM! THEY CAME HERE FLYING!!
WANT ME TO SMACK YOU WITH IT?
NOW'S NOT THE TIME FOR ONE OF YOUR FITS, MÉLIE! WE NEED TO GO! YOUR BROOM!!
YEAH RIGHT! YOU'RE GOING TO DESTROY THEM ALL!
WHAT'RE YOU DOING? LET ME GO!!
PWIII!
!!
GAAAH!
GNARK!
PWIII!
STAY STILL, WE'RE GONNA JUMP!
WAAAAAAH !!!
SHWP

WIZARDS, THIS WAS A WARNING SHOT!
THE INQUISITION HAS THE NORTHERN SUBURB SURROUNDED!
BRUSS
NORTH GATE
WHAT WAS THAT?!
AAAAH!
I DON'T LIKE THIS! RUN!
FSHHHHHHH

YOU'VE GOT TEN SECONDS TO SURRENDER YOURSELVES, OR ELSE...
...WE'LL HAVE NO CHOICE BUT TO OPEN FIRE!

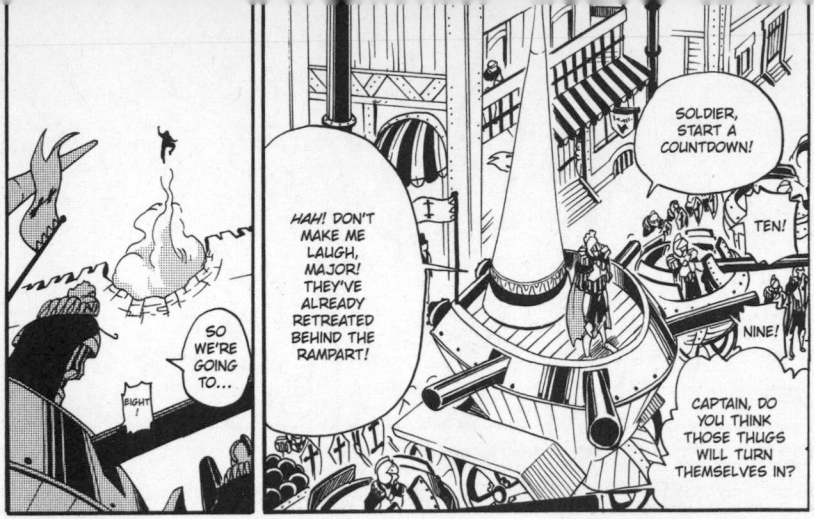
SO WE'RE GOING TO...
SIGHT!
HAH! DON'T MAKE ME LAUGH, MAJOR! THEY'VE ALREADY RETREATED BEHIND THE RAMPART!
SOLDIER, START A COUNTDOWN!
TEN!
NINE!
CAPTAIN, DO YOU THINK THOSE THUGS WILL TURN THEMSELVES IN?

TITAN PUNCH!!

FRONT LINE, CHARGE!
METEOR DROPS!!
SECOND LINE!
?!

SWP
TCH
AAARGH! I'M NOT BLIND! I CAN SEE THAT!
CAPTAIN! THEY'VE GOT A HOSTAGE!
GIVE UP, WIZARDS!
HUH?
...
...
NO, I KISS YOU WITH THIS MOUTH!!
GET OUTTA THE WAY!
OH NO! DON'T YOU DARE TELL ME WHAT TO—
SHUT UP!
NO, YOU SHUT UP, YOU BUM!
I'M GOING TO KICK YOUR BUTT!
NO, I'M GOING TO KICK YOUR BUTT, INFECTED LOSER!
WHAT?! YOU KISS YOUR MOTHER WITH THAT MOUTH?!

AND YOU, PARASITES...
YOU RAT-FACED... SONS OF... YOU THINK YOU CAN MAKE FUN OF ME?
I AM KONRAD OF MARBOURG, CAPTAIN INQUISITOR, DEFENDER OF PEACE AND THE MORAL FREEDOM AND INTEGRITY OF RUMBLE TOWN.
THE CAPTAIN'S GONNA EXPLODE!
RUN!!
I SWEAR I WILL ERADICATE YOU ALL!!

CHAPTER 12
HERE COMES A NEW CHALLENGER!

DON'T EVEN THINK OF MOVING, YOU HAIRY HARPY.
YOU WON'T GET AWAY THIS TIME!
RELEASE YOUR HOSTAGE!

CAPTAIN DRAGUNOV ...
IF YOU ARE HERE, MUST I CONCLUDE THAT YOUR PREY SLIPPED THROUGH YOUR FINGERS?
KONRAD, WHAT DO YOU TAKE ME FOR?
THAT MATTER'S BEEN DEALT WITH.
COME HERE, YOUNG MAN. NO NEED TO BE SCARED.
ALREADY ?
IT WAS NOTHING, REALLY.
BRING THE CAGE, AND THROW THOSE TWO IN THERE WITH *HIM*.
DOC!!
WHEN THIS GUY SAW US, HE HID IN A TRASH CAN.
SO WE JUST HAD TO GO IN AND GRAB HIM.
A TRASH CAN?

IF THEY START PLOTTING AGAIN, BURN OFF THEIR TONGUES WITH A RED-HOT IRON!
SHUT UP, WIZARD!
SIR! YES, SIR!
I FOUND ANOTHER NEST...IN AN ABANDONED BUILDING IN...
I WAS ABOUT TO LEAVE... HUFF... BUT WANTED TO CHECK UP ON A HUNCH I HAD AND... HAAA... I HAD TO WARN YOU... HUFF...
WHAT ARE YOU DOING HERE?! I THOUGHT YOU WERE ON YOUR WAY BACK TO ARTEMIS!

YOU HAD YOUR FUN WITH ME EARLIER, YOU LITTLE PUNK...
...BUT NOW HAVE I EVER GOT SOME FUN PLANS FOR YOU. HOW ABOUT A LITTLE BARBECUE IN THE CENTER PLAZA AT SUNDOWN?
NOT INTERESTED.
NOT ASKING!
LEAVE THIS ONE TO ME.
NO MATTER. THEY CAN'T USE MAGIC IN THESE BLACK-SILVER CAGES ANYWAYS.
WE HAVE HIS WEAPONS, CAPTAIN, BUT COULDN'T FIND HIS WAND.

DON'T THINK I DON'T KNOW WHAT YOU'RE DOING... FIRST YOU SAY YOU WANT TO KISS ME, NOW YOU INVITE ME OUT TO DINNER...
YOU'RE IN LOVE WITH ME, AREN'T YOU?
...
WOOAHH!!
YOU THINK I'M LIKE THAT?!!
TOO CLOSE, DUDE!
NO KISSING! NOT INTERESTED, SERIOUSLY!
YEAH, YEAH, "DON'T YOU DARE GIVE ME ORDERS," RIGHT? JUST A FRIENDLY PIECE OF ADVICE. TORQUE WOULD BE VERY DISAPPOINTED TO GET THAT ONE IN MULTIPLE PIECES.
DRAGUNOV, DON'T YOU-
NICE ONE, KONRAD. YOU PROBABLY ALREADY RIPPED HIS ARM OUT OF ITS SOCKET...
?!
TORQUE THE SAVAGE?!

YOU RUNNING AWAY, DRAGUNOV ?
BEING CLOSE TO WIZARDS MAKING YOU NERVOUS?
A LITTLE, YEAH...
BUT NOT JUST THAT– I STILL HAVE AN ONGOING INVESTIGATION... JUST ABOUT WRAPPING UP.
YOU'RE INVESTIGATING THE WIZARDS WHO'RE ALREADY LOCKED UP? HA HA HA!

WHO SAID I WAS TALKING ABOUT WIZARDS...?
CAPTAIN OF MARBOURG?

CAPTAIN! IT'S TOTAL PANIC OVER THERE!
A GROUP OF ARMED MEN IS TARGETING EVERY SINGLE CIVILIAN FROM THE NORTHERN SUBURB! WE CAN'T CONTAIN THEM ANY LONGER!

THE HOSTAGE, SIR?
HOSTAGE? HA HA! OPEN YOUR EYES, SOLDIER!
HOLD YOUR GROUND.
YOU, KID, UP ON THE RAMPART WITH ME. NOW.
NOW'S OUR CHANCE!
SO LET'S HURRY THIS UP WHILE THAT WEASEL DRAGUNOV'S BUSY.
HE'S NO HOSTAGE. HE'S AN ACCOMPLICE!
THIS LITTLE WIZARD PLACED HIMSELF IN BETWEEN ME AND MY TARGET WHEN I CHARGED AHEAD.
WE CAN'T TOLERATE HIM STAYING ON THE ISLET MUCH LONGER.
AND LOOK... HE'S INFECTED!

WE COULD HAVE ESCAPED ON MY BROOM... BUT MY FIT...
WE COULD HAVE MADE IT AND COME BACK TO SAVE YOU, DOC. I'M SURE WE COULD HAVE...
IT'S ALL MY FAULT!

DOC?!

DOOOOOOOC!!
...TO HAVE YOUR VOICES HEARD AND TO DEFEND YOUR FREEDOM...
!
BRAVE CITIZENS! ALL OF YOU HAVE COME TO THE NORTHERN SUBURB...
...AND THANKS TO YOU...
...
KILL 'EM!
PUT THEM TO DEATH!
...WE HAVE APPREHENDED OUR WIZARDS!!
YOU ARE ALL HEROES!
YEAAAH!!

YOUR COURAGE IS AN EXAMPLE FOR THE CITIZENS OF RUMBLE TOWN, AND A STRONG MESSAGE FOR US INQUISITORS!
YOU ARE SCARED THAT THE EVENTS THAT OCCURRED HERE 15 YEARS AGO ARE BOUND TO REPEAT THEMSELVES.
THAT A PART OF THE ISLET WILL COLLAPSE BECAUSE OF THE ILL WILL OF A GROUP OF TERRORISTS AIDED BY A COUPLE OF INFECTED SCUM...
I PERFECTLY UNDERSTAND YOUR CONCERNS AND SHARE THAT SAME FEAR! AND THOSE FEARS ARE JUSTIFIED! FOR I HAVE PROOF- BEHOLD!!

JERK! LET HIM GO!
THIS INFECTED ONE!!
HOW MANY OTHER ACCOMPLICES ARE THEY HIDING? HOW MANY MORE INFECTED WIZARDS? DOZENS? HUNDREDS?!
AN ACCOMPLICE TO THE GROUP OF WIZARDS THAT HAS BEEN HIDING AMONGST THE NORTHERN SUBURB IMMIGRANTS!

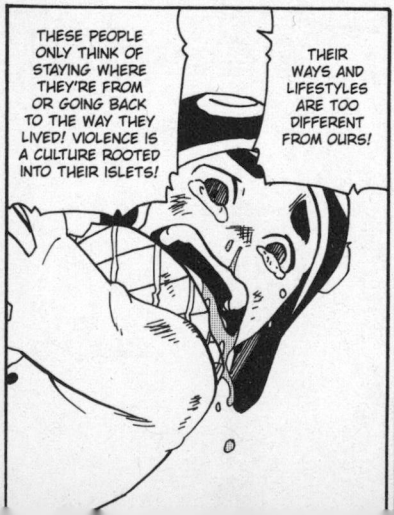
THEIR WAYS AND LIFESTYLES ARE TOO DIFFERENT FROM OURS!
THESE PEOPLE ONLY THINK OF STAYING WHERE THEY'RE FROM OR GOING BACK TO THE WAY THEY LIVED! VIOLENCE IS A CULTURE ROOTED INTO THEIR ISLETS!

AND ALL THIS BECAUSE OF WHAT? OUR TOLERANCE!!
WE'RE TOO TOLERANT!
WE'VE BEEN ACCEPTING OF EVERYTHING! THEIR CUSTOMS, THEIR DIFFERENCES, THEIR SHEER NUMBERS!
BUT WE WOULDN'T FACE REALITY, EVEN WHEN ALL THE FACTS WERE RIGHT THERE IN FRONT OF US FROM THE START!

LET'S RISE UP! AND DEFEND OUR FREEDOM!
LET'S TAKE BACK EVERY PIECE OF LAND!!
SO BEFORE THEY TRANSFORM OUR ISLET INTO A BLOODBATH AND CHASE US OUT OF OUR OWN HOMES...
...RUMBLE TOWN!!
LET'S TAKE BACK...
I AM MERELY PURIFYING THE ISLET OF THE PLAGUES THAT THE INVADERS HAVE BEEN SPREADING AROUND!
CALLING UPON WIZARDS LIKE YOU...THAT SORT OF COWARDLINESS IS EXACTLY THE KIND OF LOW MOVE THAT VERMIN INTENDING TO TERRORIZE POOR, HONEST PEOPLE WOULD-
YOU'RE THE ONE CREATING A BLOODBATH, YOU FREAKIN' LUNATIC!!
HMM... CIVIL OBEDIENCE... THIS WILL BRING ABOUT OUR DEATHS!

?
WE ONLY CAME HERE TO HUNT NEMESES!
A BUNCH OF THOSE MONSTERS ARE HIDDEN IN RUMBLE TOWN! EVERYONE HERE IS IN DANGER IF YOU DON'T DO ANYTHING!
SOLDIER! CODE VERMILION!!
THE WIZARD HAS STARTED CONFESSING!
HEY!! THAT'S NOT WHAT I SAID!!
HIM AND HIS PACK ARE HIDING NEMESES IN THE NORTHERN SUBURB!
YOU HEARD THE CAPTAIN! CODE VERMILION!!
DON'T LET ANY NEMESES LEAVE THE AREA!
LOWER THE PORTCULLIS!!
BE SURE TO AIM WELL OVER THE WALL, I DON'T WANT TO GET SHOT!
ARM THE CANNONS!
NOOO! THAT'S MY FAMILY!
YOU'RE GOING TO KILL EVERYONE! STOP IT!
BLONK
!

W-WHERE IS THIS FANTASIA COMING FROM?!
BUT WITHOUT THOSE COWARDLY WEAPONS, YOU ARE NOTHING! THE PIECES HAVE STARTED MOVING, AND YOU WON'T BE ABLE TO STOP IT! JUST LIKE MY WILL AND MY HELMET, THIS MOVEMENT IS UNCHANGING, AND UNWAVERING!
STOP GIVING ME ORDERS, VERMIN!!
I'M GOING TO DESTROY YOU!
HIT AS MUCH AS YOU LIKE!
INFECTED, CRIMINALS, FOREIGNERS– THEY'RE ALL THE SAME! THEY'RE ALL JUST VERMIN!
AS LONG AS FOREIGNERS INVADE OUR ISLET, THE THREAT WILL NOT SUBSIDE AND I WILL BE THERE TO GUIDE MY FELLOW MAN.
JUST LOOKING AT THEM MAKES ME SICK.
NO MORE RADIANT, NO MORE INFECTIONS ...
I'M GONNA DESTROY RADIANT, AND THEN PSYCHOS LIKE YOU WON'T HAVE ANY EXCUSES ANYMORE!
...AND NO MORE INQUISITION !
I'M GOING TO SMASH THEM BOTH TO PIECES!!
?!
THAT STUPID REASON OF YOURS...
...AND THAT POT YOU'VE GOT ON THAT STUPID HEAD OF YOURS...
YOU WANT TO BURN THEM ALL BECAUSE THEY DON'T LOOK LIKE YOU?!

BAG

WHAT?!
!!
NORTH GATE
IT'S...
IT'S THE CAPTAIN!!
CAPTAIN!
HE'S THE ONE WHO BEAT UP THE CAPTAIN?!
IS THAT THE LITTLE WIZARD?!
STOP!!
FIRE!
HOLD IT!!
MAJOR, WHAT DO WE DO?
YOU HEARD THE CAPTAIN! THAT WIZARD IS WORKING WITH NEMESES ON THE OTHER SIDE!
START SHOOTING! FOR THE CIVILIANS' SAFETY!

KRUSHHH
AAAAH!!
WE DON'T KNOW WHERE THE NEMESES ARE!
IF YOU FIRE, YOU'LL KILL EVERYONE!!

FIRE!
CAPTAIN, WE SHOULD RING THE EMERGENCY EVACUATION BELL FIRST, TO SPARE AS MANY–
FIRE!
WOOOM
THAT CANNONBALL MUST NOT CROSS THE WALL!
SKULL POKE!!

SCREW IT, EVERYONE'S COUNTING ON ME, SO...
HUFF... ONE ARM ISN'T ENOUGH...

IS HE ONE OF THE HORNED GUY'S ALLIES?
IT'S ANOTHER WIZARD!
HE ABSORBED ALL OUR CANNON-BALLS!!
W-WHAT IS IT THIS TIME?

IT'S TIME YOU AND GRIMM HAVE A HEART-TO-HEART, MY HORNED FRIEND.
GRIMM SUGGESTS YOU DON'T LIE- THE BANDAGE I WRAPPED AROUND YOUR ARM IS TRANSMITTING YOUR HEART'S BEATS...
WHAT IS THE FLUTE PLAYER LOOKING FOR?
I HAVE NO IDEA WHAT YOU'RE BABBLING ON ABOUT! BUT IF THOSE PEOPLE BEHIND THE WALL GET HIT BY THE INQUISITORS, I SWEAR I WILL KICK YOUR BUTT!!
HOW WOULD I KNOW?! I DON'T EVEN KNOW WHO THAT IS!
CANNONS ARMED!
WHY DID SHE LEAVE HER NEMESES TO YOU THE OTHER NIGHT?
WHAT IS HER GOAL?
I DON'T KNOW WHAT YOU'RE TALKING ABOUT!
ARM THE CANNONS.

MAYBE HE'S COME TO HELP US?
HE KILLED THE OTHER WIZARD?
I DON'T CARE. FIRE!
AAAH!!
HE'S SENDING OUR CANNONBALLS BACK AT US!!
AAAHHH !!

WE NEED MORE MANPOWER!!
HE DESTROYED OUR CANNONS!!
THAT'S IMPOSSIBLE!

RETREAT!!
HE'S TOO STRONG!

PWIII!
PWIII!
MR. BOOBRIE?!

PWIII!

THE PAIN SHOULD HAVE SUBSIDED BY NOW.
AND YOU SHOULD HAVE REGAINED FUNCTION OF YOUR ARM TOO.
WITH JUST A LITTLE SPELL, GRIMM PUT FANTASIA THAT'S BONDING TO YOUR FRACTURE LIKE A TYPE OF CEMENT.
THE EFFECT WON'T BE PERMANENT, BUT YOU SHOULD BE ABLE TO FIGHT NOW.
THE PIECE OF BANDAGE GRIMM PUT ON YOUR ARM WAS MADE FROM THE INFAMOUS FEATHER TREE.
...
WAIT... I DON'T GET IT.
MY SINCERE APOLOGIES.
WHERE ARE GRIMM'S MANNERS.
NO, NOT THAT... I DON'T GET WHY YOU'RE HELPING ME?
WHO ARE YOU?
GRIMM
-TEMPORARY ALLY-

YOU THREATENED MÉLIE AND DOC...
LIAR! YOU'VE BEEN TRYING TO KILL ME SINCE I ARRIVED HERE!
THAT'S MORE THAN ENOUGH FOR ME TO WHOOP YOU GOOD!
OH THAT!
GRIMM WAS MISTAKEN ABOUT YOU, AND IT SEEMS YOU MISUNDERSTOOD GRIMM.
KILLER?
DON'T PRETEND YOU'RE INNOCENT! YOU EVEN BRAGGED ABOUT IT! ALL THE DISAPPEARANCES ...
HOLD ON! I DON'T FRATERNIZE WITH KILLERS!
APPEARANCES SOMETIMES CAUSE QUITE A BIT OF CONFUSION– US WIZARDS WOULD KNOW...
UNLESS ...
HE'S...
NO... PIODON IS A LITTLE OLDER... THE STORIES TELL OF AN ADULT MAN...
PIODON?
WHAT ?!
OH DEAR, GRIMM HADN'T NOTICED...
A HORNED WIZARD IS WIELDING FANTASIA BAREHANDED...
...YOUR OLDER BROTHER?

FSHHHHHH HHHHHH
WHERE'S ALL THIS FANTASIA COMING FROM?!!
IT'S TIME... LOOKS LIKE SHE'S DECIDED TO COME OUT OF HIDING.
WHO?!
THE ONE GRIMM MISTOOK FOR YOUR ALLY...

THE TAMER OF NEMESES.
HAMELINE
-DOMITOR WIZARD-

To be continued...

HAH! EVEN BETTER!
THE REASON I'M SO HAPPY IS BECAUSE I GOT THE RESULTS FOR OUR "CREATE YOUR OWN WIZARD" CONTEST WE STARTED IN VOLUME 1!
PEOPLE ACTUALLY RESPONDED TO THAT?!!
AND NOT JUST A FEW PEOPLE...
GOOD MORNING, DOC! YOU SEEM PRETTY HAPPY TODAY!
YOU FOUND A NICE GREEN PASTURE TO EAT?
BAA, BAA, BLACK SHEEP, HAVE YOU ANY WOOL? YES SIR, YES SIR, THREE BAGS FULL! ONE FOR THE MASTER, ONE FOR THE DAME. AND ONE FOR THE LITTLE BOY WHO LIVES DOWN THE LANE!
LA, LA, LA... HM, HM, HM...
BONUS
AT FIRST THE AUTHOR WASN'T TOO SURE...
I GOT TWO ENTRIES...
A PHOTO OF HARRY POTTER WITH A MUSTACHE...
...AND A BLANK PIECE OF PAPER... WOULD THAT COUNT AS AN INVISIBLE WIZARD?
DEAR READERS, SO MANY OF YOU HAVE SENT US YOUR ORIGINAL CHARACTERS!!
BUT FROM DAY ONE WE'VE BEEN BLESSED BY YOUR OVERWHELMING ENTHUSIASM! THANK YOU SO MUCH!!
TH-THANK YOUUU... GAH!
MAYBE JUST A LITTLE LESS...
AT LEAST TEN MILLION!

THE WIZARD WITH STRONG FACIAL HAIR!
THE NAME SAYS IT ALL.

Infection: Disproportionate limbs. This character is 7'7" and weighs 346 lbs.
Specialty: His disproportionate limbs make him a very slow fighter and not very good at magic, but his equipment and powerful attacks more than compensate for these weaknesses.
Accessories:
Ⓐ Protection Spell: Activates a defensive bubble in the case of an enemy attack. Strong point: Doesn't use up Fantasia. Weak point: After activation the spell can't be used again.
Ⓑ Glove with direct injection of Potions into the user's hand. Strong point: Multiplies the effect of any potion. Can create giant flames, ice, etc and hits depending application. Weak point: The potion only allows for three attacks.
Ⓒ Potion Boost: Moving this gigantic body and using these overpowered magic attacks all demand a lot of energy. Weak points: Very addictive and can cause dependence.
Users habituated to this must consume an increasing amount to keep up the effect.

GLING-GLING.

A MESSENGER WHO TRAVELS ON ONE OF THE FASTEST BROOMS EVER CREATED.
INFECTION: HE FALLS ASLEEP WHENEVER HIS SURROUNDINGS ARE COMPLETELY SILENT.
TO REMEDY THAT, HE'S ATTACHED BELLS TO HIS CLOTHES AND BROOM (THUS HIS NAME).

CREATED BY YOANN VORNIERE

HEY, YOU WITH THE HAT! CAN YOU GET ME THE SAME BELT? *PSST*, WHAT'S THE YOUR NAME AGAIN... HEY, *RONNY APLENTY!*

THAT'S A CRAZY CHARACTER DESIGN! I WISH I COULD HAVE COME UP WITH IT!!

Name: Canele44e

Healer specialized in potions

Infection: She's entirely consumable, but her body slowly regenerates itself after a certain amount of time. Her blood smells like strawberries, her skin of almond paste, etc.

Useful when the pantry is empty or when you forgot your snacks! Nevertheless, her body is quite small, so her "guests" are never completely full.

CREATED BY VELKIA

A deliciously cute face.

OOH, CUTE!! A SWEET DRAWING AND VERY EXPRESSIVE DESPITE THE YOUNG AGE!

LOCUS
LOCUS IS AN OLD INQUISITION SOLDIER. HIS AIRSHIP AND THE BRIGADE HE WAS IN WERE ERADICATED BY A NEMESIS. HE WAS THE ONLY SURVIVOR. THOUGHT TO BE DEAD, HE QUIT THE INQUISITION AND BECAME A SOLITARY WIZARD.
HIS CONTACT WITH THE NEMESIS MADE HIM LOSE HIS SIGHT.
HE USES HIS MAGIC RAKE TO FLY AROUND, BUT ALSO USES IT AS A WEAPON. HIS MAGIC HELMET ALLOWS HIM TO MORE EASILY PERCEIVE AND SURVEY PEOPLE'S MINDS.
CREATED BY SOUTHIPHONG ANOULITH
THIS CHARACTER DESIGN IS ALSO REALLY WELL DONE! LOOK AT THAT ARMOR!! AND THE CRAZY CAPE! OOH LA LA...
CREATED BY SÉBASTIEN VASTRA
AN ILLUSTRATOR FRIEND OF MINE WAS NICE ENOUGH TO JOIN IN ON OUR CHARACTER CREATION CONTEST AND CAME UP WITH KINUITO. I DON'T HAVE THE SPACE TO ALSO PUT THE TEXT THAT GOES WITH HIM, BUT IT'S AS AMAZING AS THE DRAWING WITH AN INCREDIBLE BACKSTORY FOR THE CHARACTER...
I WAS SO SURPRISED, I HAD MY SOCKS AND MY BOXERS BLOWN.
WHY AM I NOT DRAWN WITH ALL THAT SWAG AND EVERYTHING LIKE THAT GUY?!
VASTRA 10-2013

History:
Octo is a young man. He's egocentric and a rebellious lone wolf. He's very brave, but just slightly too self-confident. He eats fish all the time and loves sleeping in his hammock.
His favorite hobbies are surfing and fishing. His other hobby is flirting with beautiful young women. Unfortunately, that's when he always loses his confidence and ends up goofing it up when he's in front of them. And his infection doesn't help either: his hair (dreadlocks) was replaced by an octopus! So Octo can't flirt with women while keeping a straight face anymore and keeps on getting tentacles slapped in his face and ink sprayed all over him.

Powers, Equipment:
Octo controls water. He can summon large quantities of water, or even sharks, using his parchments. All of his equipment (parchments, maps etc.) are kept in the turtle shells that he uses as a backpack. Smaller turtle shells are used to hold his potions. He fights Nemeses using spells, his blade and his knuckle-dusters made from shark teeth. He uses his surfboard instead of a magic broom, surfing on top of magic water that floats underneath his surfboard as he moves.

AND A SECTION DEDICATED TO THE READERS' QUESTIONS!
DOUBLE GAH!
PERFECT, LET'S DO ANOTHER CONTEST THEN, MY LITTLE BIRDS!
GAH!
THANK YOU EVERYONE FOR ALL YOUR ENTRIES AND YOUR SUPPORT!! THANKS TO YOU, I FEEL EMOTIONALLY REGENERATED!
READY TO FACE ANY DANGER!
ALSO, DON'T HESITATE TO SEND IN ANY QUESTIONS OR LETTERS TO:
QUESTIONRADIANT@ANKAMA.COM
WE'LL ANSWER A FEW OF THEM IN THE NEXT VOLUME.
THE SIX FUNNIEST, MOST ORIGINAL OR CRAZIEST DRAWINGS WILL BE PUBLISHED IN THE BONUS SECTION OF THE NEXT VOLUME! THE WINNER WILL SEE THEIR CHARACTER REINTERPRETED BY THE AUTHOR.
SO IF YOU LIKE TO DRAW, WE WILL BE STARTING ANOTHER DRAWING CONTEST! THE CONCEPT STAYS THE SAME—COME UP WITH A WITCH OR WIZARD AND THEIR INFECTION, SPECS, ACCESSORIES AND SO ON...
CONCOURSRADIANT@ANKAMA.COM
SEE YOU LATER, MY LITTLE BIRDS!
AND BEFORE LEAVING, DON'T FORGET TO PAY THE "CLOSING THE CURRENT VOLUME" TAX. THANK YOU!
TO CHECK THE CONTEST DATES FOR THIS CONTEST, BE SURE TO VISIT THE *RADIANT* FACEBOOK PAGE!

GUEST ARTISTS

-JON LANKRY-

-POP-

-NICOLAS SAUGE-

-TPIU-

This one time when I was a kid, something strange happened to me. It was late at night and I was in my bed minding my own business when suddenly, the wind violently opened my window! An old woman on a rotten magic broom appeared and I tried to move all "Hngh...!" But nothing happened! She opened her eyes and stared at me. I tried to scream, but nothing came out. She pointed at me, the wind still roaring and the curtain flying in the wind and the windows shattered... She pursed her lips and with her mouth wide open yelled with a resounding voice, "Cigar!!!" I suddenly woke up after that. I have no idea what happened and this dream will forever remain a mystery to me...

—Tony Valente

Tony Valente began working as a comic artist with the series *The Four Princes of Ganahan*, written by Raphael Drommelschlager. He then launched a new three-volume project, *Hana Attori*, after which he produced *S.P.E.E.D. Angels*, a series written by Didier Tarquin and colored by Pop.

In preparation for *Radiant*, he relocated to Canada. Through confronting caribou and grizzlies, he gained the wherewithal to train in obscure manga techniques. Since then, his eating habits have changed, his lifestyle became completely different and even his singing voice has changed a bit!

RADIANT VOL. 2
VIZ MEDIA Manga Edition

STORY AND ART BY **TONY VALENTE**

Translation/**(´・∀・`)ｻｱ?**
Touch-Up Art & Lettering/**Erika Terriquez**
Design/**Julian [JR] Robinson**
Editor/**Marlene First**

Published by arrangement with MEDIATOON LICENSING/Ankama.
RADIANT T02
© ANKAMA EDITIONS 2014, by Tony Valente
All rights reserved

The stories, characters and incidents mentioned in this publication are entirely fictional.

No portion of this book may be reproduced or transmitted in any form or by any means without written permission from the copyright holders.

Printed in the U.S.A.

Published by VIZ Media, LLC
P.O. Box 77010
San Francisco, CA 94107

10 9 8 7 6 5 4 3 2 1
First printing, November 2018

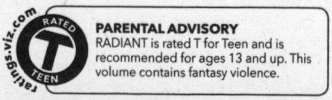

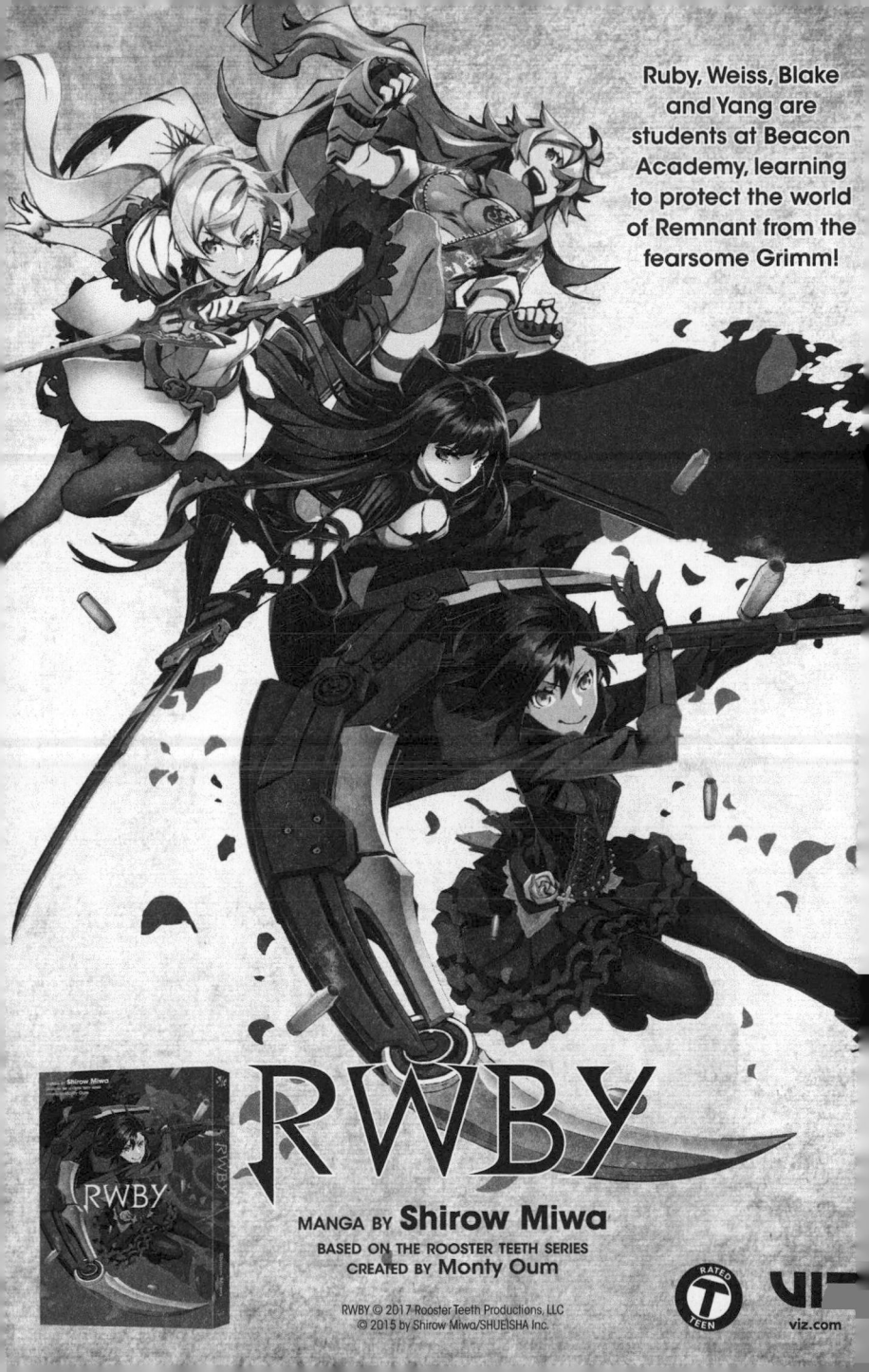
Ruby, Weiss, Blake and Yang are students at Beacon Academy, learning to protect the world of Remnant from the fearsome Grimm!
RWBY
MANGA BY Shirow Miwa
BASED ON THE ROOSTER TEETH SERIES
CREATED BY Monty Oum
RWBY © 2017 Rooster Teeth Productions, LLC
© 2015 by Shirow Miwa/SHUEISHA Inc.
RATED T TEEN
viz.com

DRAGON BALL SUPER

STORY BY **Akira Toriyama** ART BY **Toyotarou**

Goku's adventure from the best-selling classic manga *Dragon Ball* continues in this new series!

Ever since Goku became Earth's greatest hero and gathered the seven Dragon Balls to defeat the evil Boo, his life on Earth has grown a little dull. But new threats loom overhead, and Goku and his friends will have to defend the planet once again!

viz.com

DRAGON BALL SUPER © 2015 by BIRD STUDIO, Toyotarou/SHUEISHA Inc.

THE ACTION-PACKED SUPERHERO COMEDY ABOUT ONE MAN'S AMBITION TO BE A HERO FOR FUN!

ONE-PUNCH MAN

STORY BY ONE | ART BY YUSUKE MURATA

Nothing about Saitama passes the eyeball test when it comes to superheroes, from his lifeless expression to his bald head to his unimpressive physique. However, this average-looking guy has a not-so-average problem—he just can't seem to find an opponent strong enough to take on!

Can he finally find an opponent who can go toe-to-toe with him and give his life some meaning? Or is he doomed to a life of superpowered boredom?

ONE-PUNCH MAN © 2012 by ONE, Yusuke Murata/SHUEISHA Inc.

www.viz.com

Black ✤ Clover

STORY & ART BY YŪKI TABATA

Asta is a young boy who dreams of becoming the greatest mage in the kingdom. Only one problem—he can't use any magic! Luckily for Asta, he receives the incredibly rare five-leaf clover grimoire that gives him the power of anti-magic. Can someone who can't use magic really become the Wizard King? One thing's for sure—Asta will never give up!

www.viz.com

BLACK CLOVER © 2015 by Yuki Tabata/SHUEISHA Inc.

A PREMIUM BOX SET OF THE FIRST TWO STORY ARCS OF ONE PIECE!

A PIRATE'S TREASURE FOR ANY MANGA FAN!

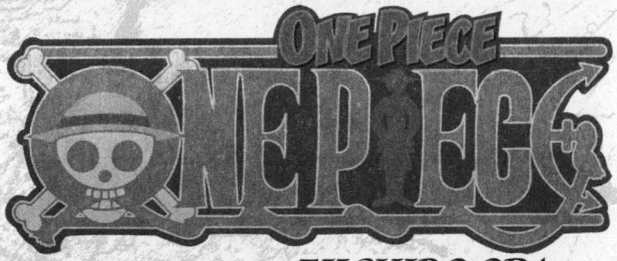

STORY AND ART BY EIICHIRO ODA

As a child, Monkey D. Luffy dreamed of becoming King of the Pirates. But his life changed when he accidentally gained the power to stretch like rubber...at the cost of never being able to swim again! Years later, Luffy sets off in search of the "One Piece," said to be the greatest treasure in the world...

This box set includes VOLUMES 1-23, which comprise the EAST BLUE and BAROQUE WORKS story arcs.

EXCLUSIVE PREMIUMS and GREAT SAVINGS over buying the individual volumes!

WWW.SHONENJUMP.COM

ONE PIECE © 1997 by Eiichiro Oda/SHUEISHA Inc.

ratings.viz.com

www.viz.com

ASTRA LOST IN SPACE

CAN EIGHT TEENAGERS FIND THEIR WAY HOME FROM 5,000 LIGHT-YEARS AWAY?

It's the year 2063, and interstellar space travel has become the norm. Eight students from Caird High School and one child set out on a routine planet camp excursion. While there, the students are mysteriously transported 5,000 light-years away to the middle of nowhere! Will they ever make it back home?!

VIZ
viz.com

RATED T TEEN

KANATA NO ASTRA © 2016 by Kenta Shinohara/SHUEISHA Inc.